Noah

Noah

K C Dayton

Copyright © K C Dayton 2023.

The right of K C Dayton to be identified as the author of this work has been asserted by her in accordance with the copyright laws.

All Rights Reserved

No part of this publication may be reproduced, transmitted, or stored in a retrieval system, in any form or by any means, without permission in writing from the copyright holder.

To my loves, all three.

Acknowledgements

To my soul family, on earth and in heaven.

Thank you for being with me on this amazing journey called life and thank you for always knowing that it should be fun. Our energy and love for one another will always exist and for that, I am ever grateful.

About the Author

Bought up to by a single parent in the harsh streets of inner city Birmingham, K C Dayton imagined her life much differently than what presented. From a French, Irish and gypsy lineage, it's no surprise that the outer world and spiritual realm has featured so highly in her life and writings. Challenged by the loss of her parent at such a young age and with suspicions surrounding his death, Dayton's quest for answers and inquisitive mind has borne a book detached from the outer world, which casts a light on the question, what is this life really all about?

Contents

Acknowledgements	vii
About the Author	ix
The Dark Side	1
Devon	11
The Girls & Kingsbridge	19
Back to Ordinary…	27
The Voice	40
Layla Willows	48
Everything Changes Forever	59
X – Carridion	69
Regroup	89
Preparing to Leave	102
It's Time	112
Getting On	150
The Letter	162

Chapter One

The Dark Side

Upon the mattress on the tiled apartment floor, Noah lay. Eyes tightly shut, fists clenched, knuckles white, blood visibly pulsing through his veins.

At this precise moment, he would give anything to escape this bone-chilling terror he was surrounded in. Just to feel free. To exit this existence that engulfed him. But he wasn't free, and he didn't feel able to exit.

For six excruciating hours, he had been amongst the dark side in this spiraling motion that made him feel sick. He was, in fact, suspended in mid-air, arms flailing as the energy-sucking entities fed off his pure life force. Making breathing almost impossible, Noah knew death was imminent but that would undoubtedly feel better than this. At what felt like the depletion of any last strands of energy, Noah began to notice that his earthly reality was slipping away. His body was rendered immobile. He was incapable of opening his eyes or moving. It felt like a force was pinning him down to the bed and this whole other dimension he had entered, resulted in the Earth's reality no longer being his predominant existence. This world full of torture, in the pits of what can only be described as hell, had become his unfortunate destiny.

Beads of sweat dripped down off his chest and onto the expensive white sheet beneath him. The mattress now damp from the excessive strain on his young seventeen-year-old body.

Slowly, losing the strength to fight, Noah began to surrender. Not to the entities, the dark side, or the fear-driven voices in his head but to the only thing that could help him. The one thing most only access in times of sheer desperation; Prayer!

'Please help me. Please! Please help. Please. Please help!' He said repeatedly, but as he struggled on only the odd word came out.

In his mind, he was screaming out but it was as if they had rendered his whole body incapable.

No help came, and nothing appeared to change!

He felt himself spinning further down into this never-ending tunnel of darkness. His pleas appeared in vain amongst this place. He was now certain he was in hell, and he thought there was a great possibility he would never get out. Maybe this is what they had been referring to all along. How bad of a person had he been, he thought.

Desperate, Noah repeated the prayer again and again, but still, all he could manage to vocalise was 'Me'.

He slowly looked down, too scared up until now. Beneath him lay the volcanic explosions. The noise was tremendous and the fire could be felt at the bottom of his bare feet as he remained suspended mid-air in what seemed a no man's land. He realised that this had got to be one of the worst kinds of torture to find oneself in.

Hours past, Noah could still sense the real him in this existence. He could still distinguish his voice in his head but struggled to recall the past or his family and friends. It was as though they were being wiped from his memory, yet he felt they were missing. Tears started to fall down Noah's cheeks.

Noah continued to call on God. But who was he to ask for God's help? Why would they help him, he thought, but he continued in desperation.

As if by divine intervention, he started asking for Mary instead.

Noah knew he needed her, but she had every right not to bother helping him. He hadn't been an advocate for her or the family anytime recently. He hadn't been to church for years but like his life depended on it; which in theory it did, he turned to her. But this time it was as if he was calling out to his own mom.

'Mary, Mother of God, please help me! I will never deny you or God or Jesus again.'

Nothing! Just entities continuing to draw on his last strands of energy.

'In the name of Jesus, you will not take me.' Noah muttered to himself.

And there in that moment, as though the heavens had opened, the shift occurred. Something had changed. Maybe Mary was there somewhere willing to help him. This thought alone filled Noah with a glimmer of hope. Noah continued to repeat the words, and this time the words started coming out of his mouth. Suddenly, it felt like the whole world had opened up and transformed itself to help him. Noah felt a surge of much-appreciated cool air flood in from above as though someone had just removed the lid to a manhole he'd been stuck down. Strands of light bounced off the sides of the gnarly grey rock surrounding him. Noah looked across and saw water glistening as it ran down the walls. Noah's focus fell onto himself, and the small entities latched onto him. He gasped for breath as he caught sight of them. Their faces were distorted and covered by rough, leathery skin. They had small sharp needle-like teeth that were entering in and out of his skin, causing their jaws to be covered in his blood. Their tiny eyes shut as they purred like kittens contented by the feast they were lavishing on. Noah felt chilled to the bone. He felt weak, in pain, and sad all at the same time. He wanted out of here, this world void of love on any level. From his weak and exhausted position, Noah used what energy he had left to lift his head.

It was then that he saw her hovering there just outside the entrance as though evaluating the situation. Light seeping through her colourful iridescent feathers. An image that was breathtaking! A beautiful, mighty-looking dragon!

Poised and ready to attack!

A surge of life force re-entered Noah, and the change disturbed some of the entities sucking off his body. Some reluctantly seized their grasp to look up.

The name Mari flickered through Noah's mind.

Noah then got the impression Mary wanted to be called Mari. This slight misinterpretation of her name hadn't pleased her, so Noah began to say Mari over and over again. Barely audible as his voice was so weak, he noticed as he chanted, another surge of life-giving energy engulfed him.

Suddenly, the tunnel became almost black again. Mari had spread her wings so wide that she covered the light on the entrance to the tunnel. Noah instinctively dropped his head as she unapologetically flew down towards him. Wind flooded in with her and an intense heat filled the air as she swerved right next to Noah, blasting a mouth full of fire and roaring in sheer anger at the benevolent creatures that dared to take her on. A few of them fell away down towards the fire beneath, but surprisingly some were still so embroiled in feeding off him that they refused to release their grip.

Blasting again with a side-to-side glance of her head, their rough, scaly skins singed, but that was all. Indestructible like cockroaches!

Noah felt her huge soft wing brush along his arm as she swung around, striking the remaining entities in the face with her beak.

Everything slowed right down. She hovered at Noah's side. Half a dozen entities still had a grip, some on his shoulder, and some on his chest. The pain was almost unbearable.

Now, as though highly impatient and furious, Mari let out a sound he'd never heard before. It came from the depths of her spirit, telling them to release him once and for all. Her voice, this time, made the tunnel walls shake as she blasted the surfaces again with her fire mouth. Finally, they all began to back away into the darkness, disappointed that she'd turned up. One of the entities floated at the entrance to the black hole they'd come out of. He stared at Noah and Mari for what seemed like an eternity, but as though thoroughly pissed off now, Mari got right in his face and just millimeters away from him. Noah watched as her large hazel-coloured eyes turned from kindness and compassion to disdain and fury. Through her wide-open jaws, she gave an almighty roar. Time stood still. The evil petulant entity slowly turned around and disappeared into the void.

Noah looked on as Mari's eyes slowly returned to calm. Heat still radiating from her jaws, she lowered her head slightly as though exhausted by her effort. Calmness and still fell over them, and Noah felt a genuine warmth towards her.

She looked at him. Her eyes filled with love and compassion. He tucked his head towards her wing and she pulled him out of there. Removing him from the world, he didn't belong. Doing the one thing a Mother would do, rescue her Son!

Upon the mattress on the tiled apartment floor, Noah could feel the dampness of the sheet. His spirit had been placed back into his body, fragmented but fully back in his earthly form.

Silence prevailed.

Light seeped through the blinds, penetrating Noah's eyelids. He became conscious of his breathing and he could sense that it was around rush hour.

With his eyes still closed, he realised he was shivering. The sweat cooling on his body was making him cold. Noah's thoughts turned to Mari. Where had she gone? She wasn't like the woman he'd been taught about at school; the gentile, meek mother of an extraordinary boy. She wasn't even a woman for a start, or at least the version he had witnessed wasn't. Her presence was far more dynamic than he'd been told. He had witnessed her as the commander of the dark side. The driving force over their wayward behaviours. Fearless!

Noah wondered if it was his faith that had summoned her, although he never particularly felt a belief in God. Maybe his declaration never to deny her or God again made her appear, or maybe his asking alone was enough. Either way, he knew his life wouldn't be the same again.

Noah opened his eyes and looked up at the high ornate ceilings above. The room was bright white, and the smell of fresh paint filled the air. Noah remembered that the apartment was in a huge building in the middle of Kensington. He remembered it was the home of one of his mom's friends, Lawrence. A government advisor, full of fun but lived life at a hundred miles an hour. It was this hedonistic lifestyle that had led to Noah taking drugs the night before. They were rife amongst Lawrence's circles and, therefore seen as acceptable.

Noah couldn't hear him moving about upstairs and assumed he'd got up and gone to work.

Feeling nervy still, Noah focused on standing up. He didn't feel he could ask Mari to help him again. That would be slightly pushing it; besides, he couldn't feel her presence anywhere around him now. Maybe the whole thing had just been a terrible nightmare. It was then that he caught himself already starting to deny her, and it had only been half an hour or so.

The voices in his head and the images had lessened somewhat, and Noah felt a huge relief. Maybe it was just one of those things, he thought. He familiarised himself with where he was. Pots of paint were all along the one wall, and his clothes were in a bundle next to them. He got up and slowly got dressed, and it was then that he caught sight of himself in the huge ornate mirror leant up against the wall. Small dark bruises covered his chest and shoulders. Noah went over to the mirror to get a better look. He traced the marks with his finger.

The sight of them made him shudder and he suddenly felt the urge to get out of London. Panic started to engulf him again. He finished getting dressed in last night's clothes, frantically gathered the rest of his stuff, and shoved it into his bag.

Everything he did felt strangely exaggerated, as though his actions weren't in sync with time. He quickly left via the back stairwell and through the front fire escape.

The noise and bustle of the day seemed more pronounced than ever before. The speed of cars and people seemed noisier and faster than usual. The sunlight seemed excessively bright and intrusive.

Noah headed over towards the tube station, grabbed the necessary tickets and attempted to escape this world that was closing in on him.

Sat on the train, heading back down towards Totnes, calm ensued. Noah looked out at the rolling countryside and contemplated how easy life must be for cattle. Maybe I'll come back as a lamb next time, he thought.

Chapter Two

Devon

It had been twelve months since Noah had left for London, pissed off with Stella, for enforcing some rules on him. Teaching his mom a lesson by disappearing to London had turned out well...

Noah had spent the first part of the year getting over panic attacks and the second half of the year trying to convince Layla, his girl of three years, to take her place at University. Not because he didn't want her with him but because he knew her love of the arts. She was that talented, she had been offered a place at The Royal College and, for some strange reason, was contemplating not going.

Noah had told her all about what happened to him in London. He knew what he'd encountered had nothing to do with religion but everything to do with another existence.

More potent than any he'd ever heard of, and he had heard of a lot of 'hippie' shit in the past from Stella. Noah had wondered why the Vatican had failed to mention before, this side of God and Mari. Why had they always portrayed her as a human when clearly she wasn't always one? Noah knew that Mari was no meek version of Jesus or God. He had concluded that she was in fact a powerful force to be reckoned with in her own right. He knew that eastern cultures revered dragons for their spiritual power and importance, but Christianity saw them as the opposite. Noah had had a lot to contemplate since that fateful night.

In the past year, Noah's looks had changed quite considerably. In most people's opinion, he was still handsome with his olive skin and dark curly hair, but he had become more unkempt than ever before. He mainly walked around in charity-bought gear, and his hair had grown to shoulder length, which he tended to tie back.

He radiated an aura that drew people and things to him pretty effortlessly. He knew he had always been described as different as he was quite quirky like Stella.

His experience with the dark side had made him less fearful of things. How could he fear anything in this world when he'd experienced true fear?

Noah's attitude wasn't typical of a young man his age. He couldn't be arsed with drama and wasn't preoccupied with money or material stuff. He couldn't keep his mouth shut on more significant issues, such as restrictions on his human rights and freedom as he saw it. Laws inflicted by the government in the form of going to college at set times were one of his main frustrations.

Noah felt life was way bigger than most dared to think. It wasn't to be taken so seriously, and it certainly should not consist of some narrow-minded, hardly evolved politicians telling people how to live their lives all the time.

Noah knew he was a 'deep thinker' as others would term it, but since returning to in Devon, he barely cared for others' opinions of him. From a youngster, he'd always been fascinated with the afterlife. His dad had died when he was young of what seemed like a suspicious death, and since then death and spirituality had always seemed part of him. He had recently found a book under his bed that he used to write in. It read –

1. How did he actually die?
2. Where has he gone now?
3. Has he reincarnated into someone else?
4. Can he still see and hear me?

5. What if we all have one person living it out in different bodies?
6. Why, when I love someone are things either a lot easier or a lot harder?
7. Who and what is 'God'?
8. Could I actually be God?

The list went on and on.

Noah had since found out the answers to some of these. He knew he often felt like a little bit of God existed inside of him. He often felt powerful beyond words and even more so when he was out on the ocean. He felt invincible then!

Noah realised his fascination with 'death' had been a pass time. The voices he often heard and experiences with the other side had just been an extension of that.

Being different from the crowd had served Noah well. It had had its challenges at times, like always being on the periphery of the crowd and feeling detached from it all but this worked well though mostly as focusing on too many people at once was hard work. Noah kept his circle close and the main reason Layla had been drawn to him is because of how different he was. He wasn't rude or aloof but more amused than anything by people's ways. He didn't judge people, but his mind was often on other topics rather than the group's shenanigans, or their latest sexual conquests or new tattoos. Noah preferred pondering how long it would take him to influence someone to do something by thought alone. He'd got it down to nine seconds.

Noah saw things that weren't a part of this world. Heard voices quite regularly, and odd occurrences would just happen. The messages about people and events sometimes came thick and fast. Stella had told him he had the gift or curse depending on which way round he wanted to see it. Just weird shit used to happen.

It wasn't until recently that he realised others really didn't experience things as he did. One summer on the motorway, Noah had an impulse to move lanes and with some surreal clarity, he told Stella to pull over just as seconds later, a large truck wheel appeared out of nowhere and bounced across the carriageway. The Emins just watched as it passed in front of them and disappeared down the embankment. For the rest of the journey, Noah, Stella and his sisters just stared ahead in silence as if it hadn't happened and it was never mentioned again.

The Emins would lose things, and then they would just reappear. Things that were broken would be fixed a week later as though by magic. Stray or injured animals would turn up at their back door. Sightings of UFOs or flocks of rare birds migrating above their house. All sorts of weird shit!

Life at the Emins was far from normal, but then neither was Noah's choice of friends. His closest friend, Mikey Donaghy, had frequently confirmed that Noah's thoughts were highly amusing and slightly weird.

Today was no different.

'What are you doing?' Noah asked Mikey, who was currently strutting up and down the bowling green in high heels.

'Noah, you know full well that Gay Pride needs me full centre, so I'm practising.' Mikey he replied, chucking the flyer at him.

Noah looked at the leaflet advertising Kingsbridge's second-only annual Gay Pride event.

'You think those dance moves will get you front stage, main float?' Noah asked.

'Are you fucking serious? Have you seen the competition?' Mikey replied with a look of hello on his face.

'Well, that is true. They are still getting used to the fact that gay people exist, never mind gay Asians.' Noah said, laughing.

Mikey rarely let life phase him as he didn't overthink beyond his make-up, clothes, and planning his next collagen injection. His latest support of Noah proclaiming not to feel like most other people came in the form of-

'Oh really, well, let's make the most of it Shugs. I'm sure we won't be here forever.'

Somehow Noah and Mikey were good for one another. They stopped one another from being so neurotic in different ways, and most importantly, they laughed a lot. Mikey had once asked Noah to kiss him to see how well he could kiss. Noah told Mikey to do one otherwise he'd knock him out if he dared ask again. Mikey just rolled around laughing.

Mikey was one of the most way out there people in Kingsbridge and probably beyond. He was on his own path in life, which wasn't common. Noah understood Mikey's plights in accepting that he was adopted, gay and Asian, and Mikey tried to understand Noah's issues with life in general.

In Kingsbridge, the two of them were pretty well known. People were aware that they weren't a couple and locals would have a laugh with them in the shops, but visitors often stared judgingly at them walking around the high street. Mikey a mere 5 foot 7 with his noticeable transgender look, facial piercings, and full make-up coverage. Noah with his 6 foot 2 alpha male body, him on his mountain bike, and Mikey pedalling behind on his chopper equipped with front basket, bell, and water bottle.

They were an unlikely friendship, but it somehow worked. Their main similarity was that they both felt detached and somehow alone in this world. Other friends didn't understand their detachment. When they opted out of the shenanigans down at the beach, they'd shout for Noah not to leave, but he would and so would Mikey. Usually tottering behind in his heels, whinging about the sand that was now stuck in his fake tan.

Noah would always please himself no matter what, and that's one of the things Mikey loved about him.

Chapter Three

The Girls & Kingsbridge

Kingsbridge was a semi-rural town south of Devon surrounded by fields, forests, and coastal walks. The beach was a ten-minute bike ride away, and the pretty town was the type of place where the children walked themselves to school from a young age. Most of the locals knew each other; it was a comforting place to grow up.

The air was fresh and filled with the smell of the sea. It was clean, affluent, and had an energy and buzz of somewhere good to be. People were drawn to this part of the world. It was English abundance at its best. Not just because of the lush scenery and beautiful coastline but because it felt like a good place to be.

Everything was thriving in Kingsbridge, but this hadn't always been the case for Noah. A strict upbringing in inner city Birmingham had been the norm for the Emins until eight years ago. Noah knew they'd had a stroke of luck being able to transfer from their damp dismal maisonette in a deprived area of hell to South Hams. Their part of Birmingham had been a place where the smell of dirty nappies and rotting food filled the air from the garbage shoot, where curb crawlers and drug dealers trawled the streets day and night. The girls, while in their school uniforms, had been propositioned by men. On another occasion, Noah was flashed by a guy in the park, but as he was so used to life up there and weirdness, he just looked at him and replied with 'Really?'

You had to be ready to fight in the inner city. It was the only option to avoid being bullied, so despite the city improving in recent years, Kingsbridge was still a blessing.

Stella and Noah's two sisters, Isla and Daisy, lived in the social housing roads at the back of town in what would be classed as the poorer part of Kingsbridge. You could tell the social housing apart from the privately owned because they were all rendered and painted white. The Emins lived comfortably. Not with loads of surplus cash, but they always managed to acquire things. Stella would often come home with tickets for this and that or news that they had been given a week away from someone. She always managed to make things turn out well for them. She would often say, things like, the universe and angels have our backs, guys. Noah didn't know what she meant, but then he kind of did with the way their lives usually played out. Once, they all ended up living in a penthouse for a week. The rooms were as big as the whole downstairs of Coppice Close. Its beds were large enough to run at and gambol over. There was access to any amount or type of food and service. They had a chauffeur-driven car and tickets to attend London's main attractions and West End. All courtesy of Stella's friend Esther, a successful businesswoman she'd got to know at a charity ball years ago. The agreement was that Stella would use it while she was away on business in exchange for her cooking dinner at some point, which she still hadn't done. Esther adored Stella. She admired her feistiness and free spirit. She insisted on looking after the kids when Stella went away on her charity work events. She had never had kids, so she spoilt the Emins whenever possible. They'd been to St Lucia with her, and out to the best restaurants. It was just how they rolled most of the time.

Noah's house, a white-washed end terrace in the corner of a cul-de-sac, was airy and bright as Stella had had as many walls as structurally possible taken out. The downstairs floors had been tiled throughout. African rugs and bean bags were strewn throughout the place and whilst various artwork adorned the walls, drapes, and tiny fairy lights hung everywhere.

A gully ran alongside the house that went from the front to the back yard. Off the gully, a door led straight into the kitchen. Nobody ever used the front door. That was quite an Irish thing Stella had said.

People came and went through that door all day long it seemed, sometimes when the Emins weren't even home. It was like Piccadilly Circus Stella had recently said. A couple of Noah's friends had ended up living on the sofa as they'd been kicked out for one reason or another. The problem was, Noah's friends never seemed to want to leave once they were there. Clothes hung everywhere, the pet tortoise just wandered around aimlessly, jazz music was continuously playing unless Stella had a card reading to do, and then people were banished in silence to the back room. But the main reason people liked 23, Coppice Close was because the Emins always had time to listen to you and you felt seen when they did. You just felt important, you felt loved and accepted there. They always looked people in the eyes when they spoke. They hugged you if they felt you needed it, and Stella especially had a knack for holding onto your every word. She didn't stand with her back to you washing up half listening, she would stop what she was doing and focus on you like you were the most important gorgeous person in the room. Noah and his sisters had the same ways about them which is why people repeatedly walked back through their door.

Looks-wise, Stella was relatively small and unconventional looking. Shiny dark wavy hair, big green eyes, clear olive skin, and tiny freckles framed her pierced nose. Noah often saw people look her up and down, checking out her biker boots and ripped non-ironed clothes. He had noticed how they often took a second look at her face though especially when they noticed the tattoo on her neck. She was somehow fascinating and mesmerising to look at.

Stella was oblivious to such occurrences. She was usually too absorbed in what she was doing to notice such attention.

Kingsbridge was a place where there were a lot of affluent northerners who had migrated south. Other locals were forever accosting Stella as to why she spent so much time helping the newcomers to integrate. She regularly reminded them that she was once a newcomer.

Newness, wealth, and the trappings of it did not impress Stella. The labels they wore or the cars they drove were beautiful, but she was never envious. She had noticed how so many of them weren't that happy or had so many relationship difficulties. She often had moms at her little council house for coffee to discuss their marital problems or have a reading. On the outside, they looked so happy and like they had it all. Over the years, Stella had heard how some of these women's husbands held down high-powered jobs back in London but was coked up to the eyeballs just so they could do the long hours expected of them or how they always felt inadequate around their own partners. It was so sad.

A day hardly ever went by without a brand new 4 x 4 parked outside the house, and it wasn't Stella's car, that's for sure. She knew that all too often, people busied themselves planning and spending for the love of busying themselves. They often didn't do these things from a happy, contented place, so the minute they'd booked an exotic holiday, they'd walk out and straight into the jewellers only to experience yet another immediate short-lived satisfaction disguised as happiness. They were lost in an illusion where they were not even enjoying all the spending and planning, as it was always what was next.

Noah had heard his mom saying, 'Does it fucking matter really if your child eats olives and fucking feta cheese and not baked beans?'

Stella had witnessed firsthand children dying from malnutrition and she knew full well the bullshit surrounding middle class snobbery and food.

Fundamentally, she was right, and she had a natural ability to cut through people's delusions. Stella wasn't scared in the slightest to speak her mind, something she had been taught by Audrey her Mama, an eccentric original 1960's hippie who lived frugally in the Scottish Hebrides despite having more than enough money due to three lucrative divorces. Stella recently asked Noah what he thought would happen if the wealthy women she knew were all dropped off in a jungle somewhere to survive.

Noah laughed.

'They'd probably cry... A lot!' Noah said.

Stella laughed at Noah's exaggerated 'A Lot!'

'Yeah, you're probably right Son but how beautiful it would be to see the real them revealed. There ought to be a production of I'm a Kingsbridge wife… get me out of here. No phone, no belongings, no make-up, no botox just the real them. Now that would be amazing!' Stella said excitingly.

Noah nodded in agreement.

It wasn't that Stella begrudged the money, clothes, cars, houses, and make-up, but she knew to be truly content, you had to be happy first and then have it all. Trappings and no scope for self-growth was a recipe for disaster. Stella knew if she wanted a new car, she could no doubt get one, but that wasn't her priority. Her priority right now was painting a commissioned piece of artwork for the Icon Gallery and ensuring she and the kids were happy and stable deep down.

Noah agreed with her about the natural version of women. He loved more natural girls. It's what first attracted him to Layla. She was very natural, quirky, and hilarious. Noah didn't think he cared much for girls until he saw her little face.

Chapter Four

Back to Ordinary…

Today was the first day back after a six-week break and it was Noah's last year in official school. No different to many other school mornings; the usual feeling of dread followed by pangs of hunger on awakening.

Mable, the family dog, was enjoying the taste of salt on Noah's face. She'd been licking for at least thirty seconds before Noah even began to register what was going on. For a few seconds, Noah had forgotten who he was and where he was; this fleeting feeling of no connection to his human existence felt great but it wasn't long before he heard the dulcet tones of his sisters who were unbelievably bickering about who got to the bathroom first.

'Just get out. I'm still getting ready,' Isla shouted.

Oh God, school again Noah thought after pushing Mable away from his face. *You've got to be fucking kidding.* His following thought was the beach and whether he'd have time to get down there for an hour before the bell went.

Noah checked the time on his phone. It was already 7:42 AM. *Fuck, no chance*, was his final thought on the matter.

'How much longer do we have to attend again?' Noah sarcastically shouted, not even knowing if anyone was in hearing range.

Stella knew exactly what he was referring to.

'Morning, Noah!' she replied. 'And one more year but technically nine months.'

'For fuck's sake!' Noah said quite loudly.

Stella briefly contemplated pulling him up on his use of language first thing in the morning but decided to ignore it.

'We all had to go Son and I really don't want any more of those truancy bills, so if you can go in, that would be greatly appreciated.' she replied from the landing, where she was trying to steer Mable away from the tortoise.

'Can the turtle not be bought upstairs, people, please,' Stella suggested.

Sarcastic thoughts regarding college continued to flow through Noah's mind, *I mean, what was the government thinking? I know let's extend the attendance age of school leavers to nineteen. Put 35 energetic, forward-thinking youngsters in a small stuffy room to sit all day and concentrate before they've even woken up properly. Get them to stare at screens, listen to boring facts and then tell them they won't get anywhere in life unless they all think and behave practically the same way and learn irrelevant information and when the youngsters get frustrated, distracted, fight one another, rebel and create riots, blame the parents.*

Noah pondered the fact that adults had suffered in the past, so now children had to suffer. *What a screwy fucked up world this really was!*

No one had been brave enough to come up with another way of living and educating. The system hadn't changed in decades and he wondered how long it would be until it did. Then thoughts started popping into his head about early and late attendance slots. *Where attending at different times of the day meant students could be more motivated. Too many early mornings were a pain in the ass for youngsters as they were tired at this time of day. There needed to be a chance to learn at a maximum of four hours at a time, as this would mean more effort and gain but in a shorter space of time. Short sharp breaks, no long lunches, and literally attending education placements for an intense number of hours so as not to prolong the day was the way forward.* Even the teachers would prefer this, he thought, *as results would reflect the benefits of shorter, more structured education slots and everybody's general happiness would be contagious. Music would play in the background constantly. Not loud necessarily, but always on,* Noah thought, *absolutely essential to living.*

This system would run shorter in the winter, whilst in the summer, the days could be longer. All the work would be done because big summer holidays would be eliminated, replaced with three-day weeks and one week off now and again. The amount of work would get covered because students would be expected to do structured work outside of school at drop-in centres. All these innovative thoughts felt good to Noah, but then they were replaced by the reality of having to get up and go to college as Stella's head reappeared around his door.

'Darling, life does appear shit sometimes, but you still have to get up out of that bed at some point.'

Like Stella, Noah was a forward thinker. He had never been a fan of conforming. Never had been, never would be! Stella did secretly hope that, at some point, he would see some value in education and its help in getting some jobs, but she did accept that this was an unrealistic hope. She knew that he was likely to attend under protest until he finally found a craft.

Noah actually longed to have been born into one of those traveller families where training horses, driving around on quad bikes and being outdoors was his form of education. Noah was creative and musical, into hiking, biking, drawing, and the ocean. It wasn't even a case of Noah not being clever. He was more than capable of getting grades, but he didn't enjoy sitting in rooms full of other people, writing, or studying. The three main things schooling consisted of. He felt his imagination was being confined and his dislike of being indoors was becoming more and more of a stress.

Noah read for pleasure only and the minute he felt he had to read or write something in order to dissect it or to get a grade, he switched off. He didn't like being told what to do and so he rebelled. Naturally!

'Just ri… dic… u… lous,' Noah bellowed in a dragged-out fashion as he sauntered across the landing to the bathroom, his boxer shorts falling down his hips.

Stella caught a glance of him as he crossed the landing and she thought about how adult-like his body had become lately.

'Don't forget to shower, Noah,' she said.

But Noah continuing with his rant and unwilling to give up the fight, ignored her and addressed the issue again.

'So because the government says we have to go so we can work and earn the country money and pay taxes, this is correct?'

Somehow Noah knew the approach taken by the government, to push and push and not rejig the whole system, was what was wrong. Kids were being treated like they were on conveyor belts to satisfy statistics and ensure funding, and youngsters innately knew this.

'Yes, Noah,' Isla said, looking up from the toilet as Noah walked in.

'Did I ask you?' Noah replied.

'Well, I'm telling you. It's up to the government. They don't want a country full of uneducated idle spongers, do they?' she replied.

'Are you going to be long? I need to get in the shower, apparently,' Noah continued ignoring her opinion on the matter.

'Umm, I don't think so. Actually yes... Err, no,' replying deliberately in an annoying way and making the decision to sit on the toilet even longer just to piss him off.

Isla was an expert at winding Noah up, both intentionally and unintentionally. She would smirk to herself whenever she felt she had succeeded in pressing his buttons.

She loved school. She loved learning and wanted to be a psychologist when she grew up.

'Just hurry up!' Noah said, retreating back into the haven of his bedroom, where the familiar smell of his room and belongings accumulated nicely.

Noah knew that parents really did not get how happy youngsters were when they didn't have to go to school. *The relief, the happiness, the immense joy of not rushing around and not having this routine created by adults for adults! I mean, the lockdown had shown us how less anxious youngsters were at not having such confinements.*

Noah had come to the conclusion that;

1) Adults liked young people to go to school so they could go to work and earn money and not have to be around them all day themselves.
2) So they would grow into adults that could also earn money.
3) Adults were always planning for children's adulthood.

It was all madness on an epic scale! *What happened to living in the moment?* Noah thought, lying back on his bed. He shut his eyes and started to daydream about leading a revolution when he heard Stella wailing from downstairs.

'Noah, are you getting yourself together as I'm going soon?'

'Yeah, I am,' he shouted back.

Rush, rush, fucking rush, he thought as he got back up and tiptoed across the landing, an act he had crafted the art of when he arrived home late most evenings.

Isla shoved past Noah in the doorway, staring right into his eyes and smirking just to annoy him.

'He's not in the shower, mom.' she shouted as Noah grabbed her mouth with his hand.

'Why are you such a little shit?' he asked Isla.

They spent a lot of their time avoiding the physical act of punching one another. Their love-hate relationship was a reflection of the mere fifteen-month age gap between the two of them.

Isla was far too mature and sensible for Noah's liking, but that was only because he often felt inferior around her. The problem was that she did speak such sense. She fitted into her place in the human world very comfortably, unlike him.

If Noah could only see how she was in fact, going to be a very important feature in his future, he may not be treating her with such contempt.

Daisy, Noah's other sister, was the youngest. She was twelve but literally ruled both Noah and Isla. She scared them both a little bit with her fierce temper and she was even known to bite and growl on occasion which was just weird. If she'd done something wrong, she would happily see the other two take the rap for it. She was lovable and affectionate, but also had extreme anxiety, a complete contradiction all wrapped into one.

Stella had often said that Noah and Daisy were two peas in a pod separated by birth. That Daisy was Noah's and she'd known this as soon as she'd given birth to her. An image Noah would rather not have in his head!

Noah came down and sat at the breakfast bar. It was more important for him to go in to please his mom than it was to go truant. He knew she was right also about the engineering course. He needed to get some grades to get on that. So attempting to concentrate on the Geography homework he should have done the night before, he sat fidgeting as he was slightly agitated this morning, to say the least.

'Noah, you have ants in your pants!' Stella said to him from across the kitchen.

Noah didn't reply as he hated the ants in pants anecdote. He thought it was ridiculous, not only because what was the probability of that ever happening but because he didn't like her referring to his pants in any way, shape or form. He also chose to ignore her because once she had said that phrase, it was always followed by a story about getting red ants in her pants lying by a river one summer's day, a story he had heard too many times. As though reading his mind, she started with the tale as Noah rolled his eyes and wondered what the hell was wrong with adults. Seriously, what were they thinking? It's just not acceptable to tell you the same old stories over and over again. *Adults should really learn to just bore off,* he thought. Noah had a theory that red wine was to blame for killing adults' brain cells completely off.

Noah was unusually and acutely agitated this morning. He'd had words with Layla the night before and clearly the mood of which he'd let slip into the following day. At that moment, Noah heard the voice.

'Noah, listen to her!' it said.

Right now, Noah didn't want to listen, so he ignored the voice too.

'Noah, listen!' it said again.

Listen? Why should I listen? Noah said in thought back to the voice.

She's going on again about ants in her pants. I cannot be doing with it, Noah continued.

'Focus on her, Noah.'

It's boring, Noah reiterated but more exasperated this time.

But somehow, the words resonated through Noah's mind, through his body and being and he found himself looking up from his work almost involuntarily. He put his pen down and turned his body towards Stella to listen once again to her ants in the pants tale. From the look on her face, Noah could see how happy she was that he was paying proper attention to her. She smiled at him, smirking with that warmth that only a person that really loves you does.

'I really need to stop telling that story, don't I, Noah?' Stella said, leaning over the breakfast bar and cupping the sides of his face with both her hands.

Noah raised his eyebrows and grinned back at her.

'Sorry, son.'

Noah was a bit taken aback by her acknowledgement of what he had just been thinking.

'It's fine,' he said.

'No, it isn't. I do need to. You know, I don't know why I keep reactivating that memory because it makes me remember a man I was completely wasting my time on during that time.'

'Was it, Dad?' Noah asked.

'Gosh, no, Noah! Your dad was never a waste of time. I had you, didn't I? It was a married man I was seeing. He was a lot older than me. I was so young and naïve back then.'

'You were seeing a married man? Wow, Mom, didn't think you'd have done that,' Noah said.

'I was so needy back then, Noah. I don't think I had much self-worth at all. It was a mess.'

Stella looked Noah in the eyes, leant forward and kissed him on the forehead.

'I'm done with that story, but thank you for listening. I know I've told you that story too many times already and I really must go. I'm late.'

Noah smiled at her.

Noah grabbed what homework he had managed to complete and headed out the side door.

Chapter Five

The Voice

As Noah cycled down the coastal path towards school today, he pondered this morning's activities. He acknowledged how he hadn't changed the condition of Stella telling the story, but he did change his feelings towards her telling it and then the whole situation seemed to change. *She even seemed to change from that conversation,* he thought. Noah found himself then enjoying the sun on his face and how beautiful the sea looked. At that moment, Noah felt invincible and Layla popped into his thoughts and how he sometimes didn't always feel worthy of her. She was so together and calm. Then his thoughts jumped to having to wake up without her and go to school and how he felt like an outsider in life generally. He watched other cyclists move past him as they engaged in conversation with their mates and noticed how they seemed to be looking forward to another day ahead. He pondered whether it was because the other lads his age just didn't think like he did and maybe he was actually an overthinking bonker type of a guy. Then he thought, maybe they had just learnt to deal with situations better than he did. He knew he was a loner at heart as there were very few people he wanted around him for long periods. He could count on one hand with whom he could spend copious amounts of time. Then, his thoughts moved back to school and horrible feelings started to wash over him.

Noah thought about the voice he heard in the kitchen telling him to listen to Stella. He didn't really acknowledge the voice, the prompts, and the impulses to do things. The voice was so familiar to him now that he rarely questioned it. He had learnt to drown it out or ignore it. He knew it wasn't the sound of his own thoughts in his head; you know, the sound of your own voice reiterating your thoughts. These thoughts felt like they were coming from outside of him but were still much interconnected. The messages came when he was least thinking but somehow ignoring them was pointless because the advice would always keep flowing, directing Noah to the best outcome even though he might not think so. They were never pushy or harmful messages but calm and soothing and Noah knew it was always there, which was why he could confidently ignore them. Noah had noticed that if he ignored the voice long enough, the messages or cues would come in other forms; signs, sounds or words. They would be anything from blatant words on a billboard or on the side of a bus to the sound of birds flying above or a song on the radio. Attention to a colour that grabs his attention after asking a question. So for Noah, it was green for yes, red for no or blue, which meant wait a bit longer. Noah had worked out this connection himself not long ago.

The universe provided Noah with as many clues as it possibly could. They were a way of life and how he functioned, but no one else knew about this interaction he had with the world around him. He wasn't stupid enough to actually tell anyone about what went on in his head.

So the messages continued to flow, often guiding him to the opposite of what he was actually thinking of doing. Noah realised that when he didn't think so much, things always turned out better.

His thoughts had bounced between negative and positive and back again, all in a matter of five minutes. He really did consider whether he was actually going mad.

Suddenly, Noah was jolted back to reality as his bike caught the edge of a pothole on the coastal path and he came flying off into the brambles at the side of the cliff edge. For a few seconds, dazed, he just lay there, bike on top of him, trying to register what had just happened. The stinging of the nettles down his left side kicked in and he quickly sat up, stinging himself even more as he put his hands down on top of them.

'Aaawww, fucking hell,' Noah shouted in frustration as he chucked the bike off his now bleeding shin. The gash was quite deep and blood dripped down the side of his leg.

The voice started again in his head and he immediately began having a conversation with it this time.

'Noah!'

'Whaaaattttt?' he replied.

'You spend so much time procrastinating about your life. You were having such lovely, satisfying thoughts about your Layla and then you started focusing on other none satisfying things.'

'So you thought you'd knock me off my bike?' Noah replied angrily.

'You knocked yourself off Noah with your wobbly thoughts.' it said.

'Oh really? So I just did that because, of course, I wanted to fall off my bike and hurt myself. How ridiculous!' Noah was saying out loud.

'It's the same as when you bang your head on something by accident; this is no different, Noah. There are no such things as accidents. If you bang your head on something, then you've been banging your head against a wall about something you've been thinking lately. What wake-up call are you trying to give yourself? What thoughts aren't serving you lately? The universe always reflects back to you what you are thinking.'

'So are you saying what happens to me in life comes from my thoughts?' he said, still speaking out loud, but this time just as a woman was walking past. Pulling her dog away from Noah, who was now sitting in a bush talking to himself, Noah threw a forced smile her way as she passed.

The voice in his head laughed and continued.

'Yes, exactly that, Noah. It is the same for everyone. What you think and feel, you get to a bigger or lesser degree depending on how you are thinking.'

Noah thought he'd have to ponder this idea as this sounded quite interesting. He took a deep breath and then sighed, contemplating getting up, resigned to the fact that he was now late anyway, so there was no point in rushing anymore.

'Who are you anyway?' Noah asked the voice.

'You're not mad, Noah,' it said reassuringly.

Okay, well, whoever they were, the voice was quite encouraging but a pain in the ass at the same time, Noah thought.

Noah looked up just as Mikey pulled up alongside him on his bike. Noah noticed he had a new pink satchel.

'Hey, buddy,' Mikey said.

'Nice bag!' Noah said.

'Aww, thanks, it's new,' Mikey continued whilst stroking the front of the velvet satchel.

'What you doing down there?' Mikey asked.

'Funny!' Noah replied, holding his hand out.

'Help me up then, knobhead.'

Mikey looked at how dirty Noah's hands were and was just about to say no but then thought twice and so held out his hand out reluctantly. Noah, with his weight, nearly pulled him over.

'Oh God, oh God, oh God,' Mikey said, stumbling and trying to keep his bike upright at the same time.

Once back up on his feet, Noah raised his eyebrows at him with a look of 'really?' and Mikey just looked away indignantly.

Whilst brushing off, Noah could see he had cuts all down his right side. He noticed his arm was bleeding as well as his shin.

'Oh, you're bleeding,' Mikey said, handing him a tissue out of his satchel.

Noah just looked at him again. 'Thanks.'

He started to wipe some of the blood and grit off before deciding that it was going to be best to push his bike the rest of the way. Partly because he now really wasn't in a rush and partly because he felt like he had no energy left to do much else right now.

'You carry on, bud. I'm not rushing.'

'Okay, babes, if you're sure?' Mikey replied.

'I'll tell Henry that your dog died,' he shouted as he rode off.

'What again?' Noah replied, half laughing, half cursing as he began pushing his bike up the gravelled path. He looked out at sea to his left. His mind calmed somewhat.

'Noah! You know you don't only exist on Earth, don't you?' the voice said.

Noah didn't reply.

'You know you have a bigger existence elsewhere, which is Earth's parallel. It's a place that flows through and around humans all day, every day, existing very independently but also very cohesively.'

Noah still didn't reply.

'Time and space are clever like that!' it said.

Noah continued to look out at the sea whilst walking. Listening but not responding. In complete acceptance of what was being conveyed and without really being aware of it, giving up the fight he'd been having all his life.

The struggle he'd created with the thoughts, the guidance and the home calling that he'd been having for a very, very long time.

Chapter Six

Layla Willows

Noah eventually arrived late into the warm stuffy classroom on the top floor of the three-storey building. Henry Roberts, Kingsbridge High's longest-standing teacher, looked up from over his glasses as he entered. Not inclined to let Noah Emins ruin his momentum, he chucked him an IPad and pointed to the whiteboard.

Noah typed in the 4th of March 2027 and for the next fifty-five minutes, he listened to Henry spout on about the rise and fall of Middle Eastern countries. Noah actually quite liked Henry. He was one of the very few he felt okay with. Henry was quite an alternative. Always looked scruffy, but he didn't seem to have that patronising super controlling air about him that most teachers had. Henry had a lot to give. Noah could tell!

Sat gazing out the window, half of his attention on what a waste of perfectly good sunshine outside, a quarter of his attention on what the scruffy but endearing Mr Roberts had to say and another quarter pondering the idea of what the actual use to his life was the history of Iraq. In fact, what actual use to his life was any history apart from a pass time hobby. It was history for a reason. *It had gone,* he thought. *Times had moved on, guys!* Should he not be hearing about time-space reality, altering reality with thought and having discussions about living simultaneous lives at one present time? This is what Noah wanted. Iraq and the surrounding areas were hardly cutting it with him or his fellow year 13s.

Each day of that week was pretty much the same. Noah dragged himself to sixth form, missing out on glorious weather and entertaining himself with thoughts of Layla.

Thursday evening was to be a bit of a change from the norm, though. Layla arrived around eight. Stella and the girls had gone out to the cinema, so they both headed straight up to Noah's room, where he was attempting to sort clean and dirty clothes from the bundles on the floor. Quite often, Layla would make herself comfy on his bed whilst he did jobs and chatted. Today was no different. Noah was excited about his new surfboard sent over by his uncle Frank, so he was chatting about that.

'Yeah, the board is amazing. It came this morning. I'll show you in a bit.'

Layla didn't respond. Noah turned to look at her and noticed she was just staring at him. Noah grinned at her and she smirked back, revealing her dimples. He stood up and threw the clothes back down on the floor and moved over to her. Leaning over her, he started bouncing the mattress, which made her laugh.

Rarely able to resist her, he leant over and rubbed his thumb over her lips so gently she could barely feel it. She grabbed the neck of his t-shirt and pulled him towards her. *She is so beautiful,* he thought. She was, in fact, the most beautiful person he'd ever seen and she just made him beam from the inside out. He knew that she felt the same about him.

Layla let go of his top and lifted her vest over her head. Noah still leant on his hands over the bed, raised his eyebrows.

'Oh okay, we are doing this then,' he said, smirking.

'Well, we don't have too,' she replied jokingly.

Noah pulled her arms from underneath her so that she fell back on the bed. Layla squealed.

'I didn't say that, did I, cheeky?' Noah said, kissing her mouth.

Their mouths wandered. Noah moved away and down to her neck, where he kissed and nibbled her everywhere as though he just couldn't get enough of her. Noah stroked her skin, following the lines of her shoulders and down her chest.

Layla undid her bra and handed it to him.

'Cheers,' Noah said, laughing and throwing it over his head.

Noah moved to her ears and goosebumps ran down all over her body. They both laughed as they stopped to look down at them.

Noah then looked up at her and licked the side of her cheek.

'Oh really!' Layla said as she grabbed Noah's face and licked all over it.

'That's it, missus,' he said as he swooped her up and then threw her back on the bed.

As she lay there, he kissed the scar on the top of her forehead and then the end of her nose. Noah sat up and took his t-shirt off. Layla raised her eyebrows at him whilst grinning. Her eyes lit up as she adored his body more than most things in her life.

'A magnificent sight, Mr Emins,' she said.

Noah watched her study him as she felt across the bumps of his chest and down his tummy. Running her finger along the band at the top of his boxers drove him mad.

Noah leant forward and started kissing her chest. He cupped her breasts and put his mouth around her nipple. Sucking on it whilst grabbing them firmly always sent her wild.

Noah could hear her groaning and she started to grab his hair, so he continued, but then she grabbed his hand and pushed it down towards her legs. Noah obliged and rubbed between her legs on the outside of her leggings. It felt warm down there. Noah slipped his hand down the front. Her knickers felt damp.

Stopping, Noah sat up and pulled her leggings and knickers completely off. He paused to study her amazing skin and her beautifully shaped legs. He loved the colour of her skin. She pulled her legs closer together as she became conscious of him staring at her.

'Don't you start being shy with me, miss,' Noah said, teasing her.

There was no way on this Earth that they'd only just met, she thought, looking at him. She felt a huge part of him.

Noah lay back down next to her, brushing her hair away from her face and kissing her forehead. They lay there for a while as she stroked his tanned back.

Layla instigated kissing again, which turned into their tongues passionately moving around in one another's mouths. Layla knew she wanted sex with Noah more than ever.

'I want to, Noah,' she said.

'Really?' Noah asked.

'Yes, I want you.'

Noah knew that she was feeling turned on as she kept thrusting her hips towards him. His hands wandered back down her body. Gently brushing past the inside of her legs. Noah started moving down her body, kissing her every inch. He wanted to kiss her everywhere. Partly because he didn't want to miss an inch of her and also wanting her to know how important she was to him, he caught sight of the stretch marks on her tummy and at the top of her thighs where her body had gained weight and lost it again at some point. He planted loads of kisses all over them as he knew they bothered her. Noah continued kissing down her thighs to her bent knees. He brushed his nose and lips against her skin as he moved down her inner thigh, smelling her familiar scent. Noah paused for a moment, pushed his hands underneath her bum cheeks and lifted her up towards him. It was as though Noah had known her body forever and this was just another lifetime of being with her. There was nothing about her or her body that wasn't perfect to him. He got so much pleasure from watching and hearing her. He could happily lick her out all day long, he thought.

She groaned as he kept kissing her and licking her with gentle strokes of his tongue whilst his hands held her bum firmly. She kept pushing her hips towards his face so that he would keep kissing her, but Noah knew how to keep teasing her until she couldn't take it anymore. He'd done it before. He knew if he didn't pay much attention to her, it would drive her crazy. Noah just kept avoiding her advances and continued to kiss her everywhere but there. Teasing her until eventually licking her was unavoidable because he, too, was getting so turned on.

Layla squeezed the skin on the top of his shoulders. He watched as she arched her back off the mattress. He loved her feeling so good and feeling safe enough with him to be vulnerable. He watched as goosebumps appeared all over her again as she revelled in the pleasure. He loved knowing it was him that could help take her to such places.

Noah gently and slowly put a finger inside of her, continuing to use his tongue on her again and again.

'Oh God,' she said as she threw her head back. Noah continued as her groaning became more and more prolonged. She then tensed so much. She gasped just before letting out a groan as she climaxed. Slowly, her body relaxed back down onto the bed. Noah gently kissed her inner thighs in a very much 'I love you' sort of way.

Noah looked up at her, smirking as he licked her off his finger.

'Noah, really?' she said, laughing.

'Yeah, really,' he replied.

He came back up to kiss and hug her, raising his eyebrows at her and smiling. Layla grinned back.

He lay next to her.

'What about you?' she asked.

'What about me? I'm fine, babes,' Noah replied

After a few moments, she said. 'Let's carry on, Noah.'

'Carry on?'

'Yeah, let's have sex,' she said.

A silence fell as Noah contemplated what she was saying.

He sat up on his elbows.

'Are you sure? There's no rush, you know!' he said.

'Yeah, I know, but I want to.'

He got back up and sat up on his knees in front of her. Layla stroked his legs and he winked at her.

Of course, he wanted to have sex with her.

To make her laugh, he grabbed her around her hips and pulled her body towards him, so she fell back again.

'Oooo. Twice. Layla.'

She laughed out loud.

Noah stroked her tummy and around the top of her thighs. She noticed Noah's hands had changed over the last couple of years into more manly hands. Even as friends, she remembered liking his hands. She loved the shape of his fingers and the smell of him. His hands were one of her favourite things about him. They were big manly hand and the veins stuck out on them.

Layla put her hand around his cock in an unexpected way.

Noah's eyes lit up.

'Easy!' Noah said, smirking

He was already hard.

She opened her legs slightly and Noah moved towards her.

'You okay?' Noah asked.

Layla nodded.

'You sure?'

'Yes,' she said and so Noah leant forward over her and gently guided himself into her. She gasped a little, grabbing Noah behind his neck with one of her hands.

'You okay?' Noah asked again.

She nodded as she closed her eyes. Noah could hear her slightly gasping next to his ear. It was a sensation she'd obviously never felt before.

She opened her eyes to see Noah looking at her, making sure she was okay mainly. As he was leant over her on his forearms, Noah could tell she was enjoying it and so he leant on his forearms and gently pushed himself fully into her. He lifted her one bum cheek up off the mattress as he pulled her in towards him and he continued to gently move in and out of her again and again. He found her mouth to kiss her as he continued to make love to her.

Oh my Lord, Noah thought. *She felt amazing!* It was unlike any other experience he'd had before. This was beyond just sex. It was a connection that was making him melt into her. Noah didn't know if he could stop himself from climaxing. As Layla relaxed into it, she grabbed his hips and kept pulling him into her.

'I'm going to come, baby, if you keep doing that,' Noah said.

'Do it!' she whispered into his ear.

'I love you too,' Noah replied as he grabbed her around her shoulders, pulling her into onto him as deep as he could.

Destiny played its part.

Chapter Seven

Everything Changes Forever

The following morning was like a daydream. Noah got up and all he could think about was the sex he had with Layla and how good it felt. He'd walked her home afterwards and he hadn't wanted to let her go. Eventually, she did go in and Noah headed back to his house. He kept reliving the moments with a big grin on his face.

'What's going on with you?' Mikey asked Noah in the food hall.

'What do you mean?'

'You? The face! The smiling!' Mikey said

'Haha, nothing, mate,' Noah replied.

As the afternoon arrived, Noah was still floating about happily in his thoughts. He was just about to nicely drop off to sleep in another of Henry Robert's History lessons when suddenly the door flung open and Mr Whittaker, the head, hand gestured for Henry to go outside.

Noah sat up in his chair. He felt uneasy and his heart was beating faster than usual. The change of circumstances in the room caused the noise level to rise and after a few moments, Henry came back in and told everyone to collect their belongings and make their way down the back stairwell. Sensing the urgency, everyone started packing up quickly and pushing their way out of the door.

'Is there a fire?' Mikey asked as he was putting his compact mirror away none discreetly.

'No, it's not a fire, but you do need to make your way straight home once you're dismissed. Parents have been informed,' Henry replied as he packed his own bag away.

All-year groups were released in military style down the stairwell and out onto the field.

'What the fuck?' was the main comment coming out of their mouths as some went to grab their bikes from the shelter. Teachers were gathered at the gates, which looked like a mass exodus pouring out onto the quiet back lanes of Kingsbridge.

The initial excitement of being let out of school early soon turned into panic as it was continually being reiterated that everyone was to go straight home.

Noah knew something really wasn't right and his instinct was to get to the girls. He jumped on his bike and shouted back to Mikey that he was going to get them.

'Noah, they said to go straight home!' Mikey shouted in his loudest but not very loud voice. 'Oh, for fuck's sake,' Mikey said as he jumped on his bike and began pedalling faster than his thin legs wanted to go.

Mikey lost sight of Noah as he tried to manoeuvre around the hundreds of kids walking home. Eventually, he caught sight of him about 200 yards down the lane. He could see Noah had stopped at the crossroads and stood straddling his bike.

He caught up with him.

'Mate, what's the matter?' Mikey asked as he lay his bike down gently on the verge so as not to scratch it.

'Aww, my head!' Noah said, leaning over his handlebars.

'Let's get your bike,' Mikey said, signalling for Noah to get off his bike.

'I can't see properly and there's a loud ringing in my head,' he said as he put his hands over his ears and crouched down on the floor.

He then heard the message as clear as the bright day.

'Noah, go home!'

'Right Noah let's get you home. I'm sure Stella will have got the girls,' Mikey said, almost confirming the already clear instructions Noah could hear.

Mikey called one of the Year 8's over, who was reluctantly walking past and asked her to take his bike home for him. She looked quite pleased with the prospect as it was such a cool girly bike. Mikey grabbed Noah's bike and started heading in the direction of Kingsbridge.

Holding his head, Noah followed and eventually got into the house.

'Where have you been?' Stella screamed, helping guide Noah into the house.

'You look terrible. Get straight into bed.'

Noah staggered towards the stairs, eyes barely open and when he got to his room, he just rolled onto his bed. The last thing he remembers is hearing Stella thanking Mikey and telling him to head straight home. Noah shut his eyes. The room began to spin. He felt nausea but felt he couldn't get off the bed to even be sick. The noise in his ears reached an ultimate high. Suddenly a wave of calm swept over him. Silence descended and everything became very still. Noah felt a release. A letting go of everything; the tension, the worry, the noise, the ill feeling. Everything! Noah's body started to jerk off the mattress. After a few times, he took a deep breath in but then resisted what was happening. He heard the voice.

'Go with it. You are safe!'

He could feel himself spiralling into a tunnel again.

Oh shit, not this, he thought. *Not again.*

Noah slowly slipped into the unconscious. He could hear Rosie downstairs shutting the door behind Mikey and then he saw Mikey out of the window quickly walking down the road. It was then that Noah became aware that he wasn't lying on the bed anymore, he was watching Mikey walk down the drive. *How am I doing this?* he thought. He looked across from where he was and there was his body, lying down on the bed whereas 'he' wasn't in it.

He looked around and he became aware that he wasn't actually standing in his bedroom. He was surrounded by light, but he was also part of the light as it encompassed him like a tunnel. It felt like being sat in front of a fire wrapped in a fluffy comforting blanket on a snowy December evening. Where he was, was more a feeling instead of a place, suspended amongst worlds.

At least... Noah thought. *It's not that dark tunnel again. Count my blessings and all that!*

From this place, the one that no longer involved lying on his bed in Kingsbridge, he could now see that Stella was standing next to his bed, telling him to just rest. He could see that his body was lying there, eyes shut, still breathing even, but *he* wasn't there. It wasn't as if he was floating in the room above his bed or anything, he was literally seeing what was going on in his bedroom as though he was watching a movie in his mind from where he was. He then realised he could focus on anyone anywhere. He focused on Layla and he could see that she was sitting on the sofa watching the news whilst frantically messaging him. Noah's attention was drawn back to his mobile beeping next to his bed. It was Stella messaging him. All of this was occurring through thought, but yet Noah felt fully aware and present.

His focus stayed on Coppice Close as he watched Stella check his phone and then leave his room, pulling the door behind her.

Noah didn't feel worried or concerned for anyone and interestingly, he didn't feel selfish about not being concerned either. This where he was, was the real him. There was nothing to be concerned about. He knew this from this place he was in.

It occurred to him how life really was all a game. A game to be played just like a game of chess. Our thoughts being the pawns that we move around to alter the outcomes. The main target was happiness which was what each and every single being on Earth was ultimately striving for. That's all life was! That was all it was about. Nothing more, nothing less!

Noah felt free. Free of his body, free of any fears which clearly he had been putting on himself as he didn't have them anymore.

Life wasn't meant to be serious or fear-ridden. He'd been putting all that stress on himself. Humans had created this epidemic based on a learnt behaviour regarding lack and competition with one another. Crazy passed down thinking from parents to children, governments, leaders, teachers, schools, and media.

Fear of idleness, fear of too-muchness. Fear of kindness, fear of loving, fear of being out of control, fear of control, fear of even fear.

Here where Noah was, felt right and good. There was no fear here.

Noah's focus came back to the space he was in. He became aware of people standing quite a distance from him down the end of this tunnel. Unable to work out their features, he just knew that they were there waiting for him. He could sense that they were excited to see him but also happy to wait for him. There was no rush to head towards them and telepathically, he knew that they were happy for him to bask and enjoy his time. There was no rush here!

Noah continued to slowly float, bodiless, towards them through this pure space, with a feeling that despite the upheaval he'd left in Kingsbridge, he couldn't help but enjoy where he was.

Noah stepped out towards the edge of the tunnel as he took on a more upright human form again. The 'others' formed around him, hugging him, patting him on the shoulder with such happiness to see him. Noah somehow recognised all of them, yet they weren't from the earth plane. It was all quite odd, but also not at the same time.

'Treigo,' Noah said, beaming.

'Brother, it is so good to have you back,' Treigo replied, grabbing Noah's hand and pulling him close to his chest. The words, the names, the knowledge just came to him, almost like he'd been given a portion of his memory back.

It felt right and natural for Noah to walk with them away from the 3D and maybe more surprisingly, it felt natural to have no real desire to return to that place either.

Stella and the girls watched as the PM announced another 24 to 48-hour lockdown due to unforeseen events.

The news showed some cities retaliating against the imposed law and some small groups rioting on the street as a lack of disclosure as to why was being enforced.

'It won't be long until the government has to disclose what's going on to gain some control back,' Stella said.

'What do you think it is, mom?' Daisy asked.

'I think it's something bigger than they've ever had to deal with before, that's for sure.'

'The government look concerned. Look at their faces,' Isla said.

'It's true. Some shit has just gone down,' Stella replied, nodding.

'I'm so glad we are not living up North still,' Daisy said.

'Yeah, it does look pretty dismal up there at the minute.'

'Is Noah okay?' Daisy asked.

'Yeah, he's sleeping it off. I'll just leave him to it for a few hours.'

Stella cuddled the girls on either side of her on the sofa as they decided to watch a movie to pass the time instead. This felt like real quality time again, like when Covid hit.

Chapter Eight

X – Carridion

Noah stepped out onto the perfectly formed grass that stretched out in front of him, breathing in the reality of what felt like home and feeling a huge relief to be back.

'Ah, home!' he said, throwing his head back and letting the sun beam off his face. A slight breeze blew across his face as if to say hi and as though it knew he needed cooling down. The land was lush and welcoming and the grass lifted up around his feet in appreciation. Everything was not only alive but pulsing with life.

It was brighter here. A similar intensity of light as where he'd just come from. As well as the moon and sun, two other planets were visible in the sky. An indigo blue one and a smaller orange oval one.

The sky was the deepest blue with not a cloud in sight

and the colours of the landscape were the richest shades that Noah had ever seen, or at least in a while. It was as though Noah had forgotten how nature truly looked. Continuing to walk up the gently sloping grassy area, he suddenly noticed how massive his feet looked. He looked down at his arms and they were all hairy and muscly with veins protruding. His skin was darker than usual and his body fit and lean. The type of body he would have wanted as an adult on Earth, to be honest.

Around his waist, there was a type of animal skin covering his modesty which he was yet to check out. He also hoped this would exceed his expectations.

The clothing felt familiar and he knew he'd worn this skin thousands of times before.

He touched his jaw and he could feel a beard. Noah felt like a boss once again.

Inside the sanctuary of his mind, in his thoughts, Noah still felt like Noah, the exact same, just a super pumped-up version of himself. *No insecurities, I suppose.*

As Noah walked with the group, people gathered around him, tapping him on the back and grabbing his arms as he walked. They were really pleased to see him and their smiles and warmth felt good.

The men were hot, even Noah could appreciate that. He smirked as he thought how Mikey was missing out and then it occurred to him that Treigo reminded him of a brother he felt he never had.

Noah looked around. He'd forgotten how stunning the Carridion women were too. Not just one or two but all of them in their own unique way. They were all shapes and sizes, colours and ages, but it was their calm, feminine ways across the board which made them mesmerising.

The children didn't have rules or restrictions and that freedom could be seen in the way they ran in and out of everyone's legs, grabbing them as they went. They were free and happy. They were native looking, almost like Red Indian ancestry.

The thing that filled Noah with the most satisfaction was that he knew that all of these people were his. They were all familiar, part of his family or closest friends. He didn't know how he knew, but he just did.

He looked into the eyes of his people as he walked and a warming affection spread between them.

As he continued to walk through, he saw a woman across the way swinging a child around. He couldn't take his eyes off her. She looked over and smiled with familarity and warmth.

'Happy, aren't they, Noah?' Treigo said.

Noah nodded, still glancing over as Treigo led him towards the coastal path.

The warmth of the sun on his face and naked chest felt energising. The turquoise ocean fell to his left over the cliff top. He had a moment of pure euphoria.

Treigo led them down past the huts and tepees, beyond where more children were playing.

Noah could see a small path leading round to the right. He knew it led down onto a sandy beach.

As they reached the beach, Treigo sat down on the sand, but Noah continued on into the warm waters, which felt like they were calling him. He dived under and swam until he felt totally free. It wasn't long before dolphins were circling him. It was as though they knew he had returned. This is how in zinc, Carridions were with nature. Everything and everyone communicated on a telepathic level.

Noah played with them, stroking their skin as they swam past. Laughing as they nudged his legs under the water. Being around these creatures was so healing. Just as Noah began to swim back to the shore, he noticed a great big presence next to him in the water. Treading water for a second, he felt a surge of the most powerful energy as a pod of grey whales surrounded him too. They snorted and circled him, projecting their magnificence onto him. Holding out his hand, one brushed as he swam by. Noah could feel the bumps on his tough skin. Time stood still as the majestic beasts pumped healing into Noah and he felt completely at one with them. They were looking after him. He felt their love for him as they gently moved him in the direction of the shore. Leading Noah back in effortlessly with the momentum of the waves.

Treigo looked on from the beach at the amazing synchronicity. He made his way into the water to help Noah out. As though rehearsed, the whales and dolphins did a U-turn. As they got further out, the largest whale threw itself up in the air as though in celebration, making an almighty sound and splash. Noah laughed as he slumped down onto the soft, warm sand.

'Better?' Treigo asked as though such an occurrence was normal.

'Well, my head doesn't hurt anymore,' Noah said, glancing at him with a smile.

'They came especially for you, Noah,' Treigo said, looking out to the ocean.

Noah smiled. It was difficult not to be happy here. The Carridions were clearly aware of the activity on Earth but flapping over it wasn't going to help.

Noah eventually sat up on his elbows and looked back out. He could see the whales and dolphins on the horizon. Noah sensed one looking back at him.

'Why do I love them but don't really miss them? The girls, I mean,' Noah asked.

'Because you know there's nothing to miss. You know there's no real separation between you and them. You know in your heart that they are all safe and heading back here eventually, too,' Treigo replied.

'So I'm not dreaming, Treigo?'

Treigo paused for a few seconds.

'Yes, you are, Noah, but not in the sense you think,' Treigo replied

Noah didn't care. He just wanted to be fully acquainted with Carridion again. He lay back on the sand and shut his eyes. He saw the awe-inspiring scenery, which included mountains that fell into the turquoise seas. The damp, humid rainforests streaming with thousands of animals never been seen on the Earth plane and the warm Savannahs where Carridions rode their horses bareback.

As Noah lay, absorbing his surroundings, he heard a rustling in the trees behind. He turned around to see two Trojans peeping out. Curious and shy!

Trojan's were horse-like but with the speed of Cheetahs. Native to Carridion, they had strong bodies and gentle nature. Noah stood up and approached the one. Holding his hand out as it towered above him, the beast lowered his head and rubbed it up against Noah's shoulder. This acknowledgement felt satisfying and once their curiosity was fulfilled, they soon turned and galloped back into the forest.

'Hungry?' Treigo asked as he approached Noah.

'Yeah, I am actually, but once we've eaten, it'll be time to discuss matters, I'd say,' Noah confirmed.

Treigo nodded.

'Certainly! Go fetch us some lunch first, though,' Treigo said, handing him a spear.

'Where did you get that from?' Noah asked.

'Oh, come on. You've forgotten already?'

'Forgotten what?'

'I just manifested it,' he said, laughing.

Noah looked confused.

'Don't worry, you'll catch up soon enough, Noah,' Treigo said, laughing.

In previous lifetimes, Noah had been taught how to search for food and live off the land.

'Remind me, Treigo. I'm a bit rusty, I think,' he said.

'Sure, no problem! So cast your intention. Feel and think about it. Believe it's happening and let the wish go. Trust,' he said.

Noah walked into the shallow waters. Put out the intention. He thought about how nice it would be too soon to be eating fresh fish cooked on the open fire. He noticed that they started to appear around his feet and swim in and out of his legs. He waited until he felt the impulse and then bam. He aimed his spear again and again.

'Bravo, brother. You've not lost it then,' Treigo shouted.

Grinning, Noah held up the spear above his head in celebration.

Noah turned and bowed to the ocean in gratitude.

In the interim to Carridion, in the formless mode between Earth and Carridion, Noah had totally lost that anxious feeling associated with the 3rd dimension. Now back in Carridion, his vibration had slightly dropped back down as he was feeling a variety of emotions again and some worry.

'There seems to be a huge panic going on at the moment. What's it about?' Noah asked as he removed the fish from the spear.

'We wanted you back here, Noah, because of what's going on, so we did help you go to sleep to get you back quicker. Legar knew a migraine was the best way to get you home.'

'Where is he?' Noah asked, automatically knowing who Legar was.

'He's back up the top keeping an eye on the changes occurring in 3D.'

'What's the real reason I'm here, though?' Noah asked.

'Well, you never really left us, Noah; that's why it seems so familiar. You'll discover who and why you're back here as time goes on. Trust me, brother!' Treigo said, smiling.

'Do we have enough time?' Noah asked.

'Earth is functioning at a slower rate than here, so we have some time to play with, yes. Us being the future. All is well, I'd say on that front!'

The night was drawing in and the temperature had dropped, so Noah and Treigo started walking back up the hill towards the tepees.

As they walked, Noah noticed a rock glistening on the side of the path in front. Treigo read his thoughts.

'See that rock, Noah?'

'Yes.'

'That in itself is a sign of how noticeable and bright just one thing can be. It's a reflection of your life and thoughts. It's telling you to pay attention to the small things as there's magic in the smallest of places and messages everywhere to help you. Don't underestimate what the universe is trying to convey to you all the time. It's giving you constant messages and answers! Even a rock can speak to you, Noah, if you allow it to.'

'Well, I wouldn't have read that message from a shiny piece of rock,' Noah replied.

'You will soon start to remember again, Noah. You will quickly realise that your thoughts are so powerful. Accept the help and what your intuition is telling you, as you're going to need it.'

They approached the large tepee at the top.

Inside, a fire roared from a large pit in the centre. Noah was in awe of how big these spaces were.

The light was dim and candles flickered everywhere around the tent. Drawings of vibrant colours covered the canvass and large cushions covered the ground. Animal skins covered the ground.

People were bustling about the tepee, providing drinks and food and entertaining the children by giving them jobs to do, such as filling up the water jugs or raking the sand.

The tepee was full of people. Women sat on the floor chatting and laughing. They looked Noah up and down as he walked past.

'This is for you, I believe,' Noah said, grinning as he handed one the spear with the fish hanging off it.

The women giggled amongst themselves.

As a Carridion, Noah was a beautiful sight to look at and they loved his returns which had been many more times than he was consciously aware of. Noah's aura was white and blue tones. He had strong, sturdy energy and turned heads because he was unlike any other Carridion member. The pure universal energy flowing through him was of ancient lineage, a make-up of ancestral masculine energy so powerful that others were just drawn to him. When up to speed, he felt safe and pure to be around. He oozed certainty.

Noah had become Noah from centuries of lifetimes of questioning and exposure to many experiences and choices. A loss of ego, so others' opinions and attention were mostly irrelevant. It was his ability to move forward and a knowing that there was more to him than just the physical and brain that had led him to this exact place. He had clearly been doing better than he was giving himself credit for in the third dimension.

Treigo signalled for Noah to go towards an opening beyond the main tepee. As Noah followed, two small boys ran up to him, grabbing his hands and running around him laughing. Noah smiled and looked across at their mothers. He caught the eye of the one he'd seen earlier.

'Chamelesen,' Treigo said in their mother tongue to the boys. The boys ran back to their Mothers.

'She's beautiful, isn't she?' Treigo said, clocking the synchronicity of the moment.

'Indeed,' Noah said, smiling, hardly able to take his eyes off her.

'All will be revealed, Noah. Now come!' Treigo replied.

In the adorning tepee, Noah spotted Ledar over in the corner with his arms stretched out, fully waiting to greet Noah. Noah went straight over to him like a son to his Father. They threw their arms around one another and embraced, swaying from side to side.

'My boy!' he said

'It's been a while, I believe,' Noah said

'No, my beautiful boy. We have never been more than a thought away from you,' Ledar said. 'Sit, sit,' he continued, directed towards the seating.

'Get this man a drink and some wholesome food. He deserves a feast,' he continued.

The energy was buzzing and the people he intuitively knew already somehow.

The seating surrounded one single flame in the centre that sat on a high stand above a glass plate. Water trickled down from high up in the tepee, forming a triangle around the candle. The trickling of water from the edges made a soothing sound as it landed on the glass.

'Welcome home, Noah,' Ledar said and everyone smiled and nodded in agreement.

'Right, whilst we wait for the refreshments, let's get down to business. I see you've left quite a precarious situation back there. Now, you have a task Noah, which is to inform humanity of the bigger picture. It's not one that many have been able to achieve and you must bear with us on the details as we are still working with the 3D over the ins and outs, but we are going to be taking you in your mind to see things that will affect the way you function ahead. Understand so far?' Ledar asked.

Noah looked intrigued.

'I'm to return?' Noah asked

'You will be, yes, but only in thought right now,' Ledar replied.

'But…' Noah continued.

'Listen, Noah,' Ledar said, interrupting.

'I am not going to lie. It's likely that you're going to be pushed to what feels like beyond your limits, but you must keep, above all else, your trust and faith in X. If you don't, we feel it will be detrimental to you, us and beings back there. It is time, son, to only focus on what is wanted, not what isn't wanted,' Ledar said.

'I get you,' Noah said.

'The others have been focusing on the work you have to do and what is maybe possible. They know you will be even more powerful and focused, able to concentrate on your own guidance, which in turn will serve the others back in 3D,' Ledar said.

Noah nodded.

'You are loved beyond imaginable and you know we would never leave you and have never left you, right?' Treigo said.

Noah didn't reply. His heart started thumping and he started to sweat as feelings of anxiety began to sweep over him. The elders picked up on his thoughts.

'Noah, try not to worry. Worry only exaggerates the problem that you think you're going to have. We are with you all the way, but you need to remember one thing, you will need to focus on only what you want and expect it to come. This is the golden rule!'

'Okay,' Noah said hesitantly, gulping.

Ledar continued, 'Now, Noah, many people have come before you and they have helped in propelling humanity to a higher level. We are expecting that you will be the next figure to do this when you go back.'

Noah looked confused. 'Do you really know who I am? I live in a poorer part of an affluent town in a council house in a one-parent family. I know I'm different, but there is still a part of me that questions all these goings on in my reality. Now you're telling me I'm the next biggest thing since Jesus or the equivalent. Come on guys, seriously?' Noah asked.

'Not just Jesus Noah, his mother, Buddha, Gandhi and all the psychics and magicians. In fact, any of the energies that have been able to see through the human experience and since when has being rich or poor made someone qualified in wisdom or purity?' Triego said, laughing.

Noah shook his head. Not laughing!

Noah just looked around at them, thinking they were slightly fucking mad.

'Don't worry, Noah! This maelstrom will lessen. By the time you leave here, your sense of who you really are will have returned fully and you will be ready. That feeling you had in the tunnel will come back, but first, we need to reflect on two scenarios that occurred whilst you were on Earth. Shona, would you like to continue?' Ledar said.

Shona was a woman of about thirty something. She was stood a bit further away by a large oak table which had holographic screens above it. Other Carridions were in and out bringing food and drink. Noah noticed how serene they were. Barely noticeable.

'Noah, hi!

Noah nodded at her.

'Okay, so we've noticed that life in 3D functions similarly to Carridion, but its people have become very confused and very disconnected. They have made being happy difficult and fleeting and negative easy and normal. Stress is a sign of progress and working hard whilst calm and content is seen as lazy. Humans associate the ending and separation of things with sadness and negativity. They appear overall to have lost all faith and connection to the universe and their guides. Would you agree so far, Noah?'

'Indeed,' Noah replied.

'They've forgotten that nature, the trees and the birds whisper messages. That nature comforts and heals. They have forgotten the power of harnessing their surroundings and how to call for help. They've forgotten that there is no need for verbalising thoughts all the time. Everything was transferring desires and everything was being answered without having to even speak about it. The power of not speaking about things had long been forgotten. They'd forgotten that everything they wanted was coming and the signs of it arriving were around them if they'd only just believe. We have noticed that the indigenous people have not forgotten, but the western world is certainly torturing themselves on a daily basis by denying their own innate guidance to the higher dimensions. We have noticed that the younger generations especially know that they aren't meant to be part of a matrix that controls them.' Shona flipped the screen around to show Noah an image of protesters in the Middle East regarding a recent injustice. 'Humans innately know they are more powerful than they are being led to believe. They know they have gifts and abilities beyond their current living conditions and the reasons why so many are struggling with what they call anxiety and depression is because of this shutting down of their natural abilities. Gifts from the universe are actually passed down from their ancestors. They know that they are way, way more powerful than they are able to express or given credit for. They feel it inside of them. They have a fire in them, burning, screaming to be let free. The nearest they get to experience it, is loving one another, which is why so many people are drawn to forming bonds and sexual relations. The next is exercise and competition, as it releases tension and pent-up energy. They are trying hard to reconnect to their own selves, but it just isn't working or isn't sustainable. They need to go within themselves, not outside of themselves. Since being there, Noah, your vibration level has dropped from the usual nine hundred to six/seven hundred hertz frequency. It will rise again to what it needs to be to complete the next phase, but there is a lot of work on one certain topic that needs to be done first.'

'What's that?' Noah asked

Ledar stepped in.

'We shall discuss further shortly. Food seems ready. Let's convene again after eating.'

Noah stepped outside. He thought of Layla and whether she would be worried right now. He remembered their encounter, which seemed ages ago now. He knew she was special. Even from here, he knew she was part of him.

The stars stood out amongst the dark blue backdrop. Noah wondered what the other two planets were. The whole experience was really intense, yet he felt at home, so it was quite a paradox.

Chapter Nine

Regroup

'Lemme send Epione!' Ledar said.

Noah innately knew as he shut his eyes and concentrated. Everyone in the circle focused on the flame until it became mesmerising, and then they closed their eyes. A bright light appeared as their visions were led by Noah's focus. From him, they could all see collectively what was happening.

Ledar started tapping his palm on a drum and began chanting. Noah felt like entering a trance-like state, yet he was still very aware of his actions.

The others focused on Noah, who could feel his body swaying back and forth as he sat cross-legged on the floor. The drumming quietened, and Noah opened his eyes to view his past - when he was sixteen.

'What is happening here, Noah?' Treigo asked

'That's Katie and Miles. I'd made friends with them at some party. Katie took a liking to me. She was quite a bit older, about twenty-one, maybe.

She and Miles had asked me to join them one night for drinks before heading out, so I went to their place. Upon arriving there, I crossed Miles on the steps as he was leaving the house to go get some smokes. Katie invited me in.

As you can see, Katie was flirtatious. She put her hand on my waist as I got a drink, came close, and kissed me when we started talking.

Long story short, whilst Miles was out, she basically seduced me. Do we really need to look at this scenario?' Noah asked

'You have led us to this scenario, Noah, not the other way around. Stay with it; there'll be a reason,' Ledar said

'So she touched me like no girl has ever touched me before. She took my trousers down and put me in her mouth. Fuck, was she hot! I admit I fancied her, but I knew what we were doing was wrong. After it finished, I just left. As you could see, I was anxious and couldn't get out of the place quick enough.'

'You're about sixteen here, Noah?' Shona asks.

'Yeah, just turned sixteen,' Noah replies.

'I remember just leaving afterwards. It was never mentioned again. I felt so bad for Miles and couldn't really speak to her anymore.'

'Okay, well, we think this event has been highlighted because it is stuck in your energy field as a time when you did something out of character and was completely led by your sexual energy. You felt ashamed, yet it wasn't all your fault, but this progressed into further destructible behaviour.' Ledar confirmed.

'Yeah, I didn't like that period when I was heading to festivals up and down the country, taking drugs, drinking loads, and forming meaningless relationships with strangers,' Noah said.

'Your energy was getting corrupted as you mixed yourself up way too often with lower vibrations. Sex especially does that,' Treigo said.

'I soon realised when I returned to Kingsbridge that I wanted less of that hedonistic excitement and maybe a proper girlfriend. It wasn't long after that actually that I met Layla, but she didn't want anything to do with me for ages, probably because of my lifestyle.'

'Everything happens for a reason and in perfect timing. If you think you want something in your life, Noah, and it hasn't appeared, it is because it isn't the right time for it to appear,' Ledar added.

'I do know that what I thought I wanted back then has turned out not to be what I actually needed, and better things have come,' Noah said.

'Exactly; you humans usually want too much or don't think you deserve them. The minute you give up on the idea and live without it is when it makes no difference to you whether you have it or not, then it appears. It has to! That's the law of attraction.'

Noah raised his eyebrows. Impressed with their overall insight and lack of judgement on what they'd just seen regarding Miles and Katie.

'Okay, second scenario, please.'

Ledar signalled to focus. Noah could see himself lying on the mattress in Kensington.

'Oh gosh, this. One of if not the scariest times in my life so far,' Noah exclaimed.

'We will go through this briefly here, Noah. There is another part to dealing with this that will need to happen as it's not as straight forward as you'd think, but for now, explain to us what happened here?' Ledar said.

Noah could see the image of the woman with a small child he spotted on his way into Carridion. The same woman he saw earlier in the tepee next door.

'The young mother, Noah, the one you couldn't take your eyes off.'

'Yes,' Noah said

'Who are they?' Treigo asked.

'I'm not sure. Who are they?' Noah replied.

Noah then saw himself and Layla back at his the other night.

'I'm seeing Layla. What's that got to do with them?' Noah asked.

'Yes. Who's the woman?' Treigo asked once again.

Noah paused for a few seconds and took a deep breath in.

'No way!' Noah replied.

Treigo knew Noah had got it.

'Yes, Noah.'

Silence fell in the circle. The others waited for Noah.

'But I'm here. How can I be out there too?' Noah asked.

'You're not.' Noah turned to look at Shona. 'That's someone else she's with,' she continued.

Noah felt jealousy rising in his body.

'Don't go there, brother. Low vibes!' Treigo said.

'Different time frames,' Shona answered.

'The woman here is the expanded version of Layla. The future version so to speak, so she chooses differently,' Treigo said.

'When you imagine a certain outcome in 3D, it occurs straight away here in Carridion,' Shona explained.

'That's why I can't take my eyes off her!' Noah said.

'Yes, exactly! So when you are missing someone or something, Noah, it's because that's happening some place, somewhere, but you are just not feeling connected to it,' Ledar said.

'Wow!' Noah said, smiling.

His thoughts went back to the woman on his arrival. She did look so familiar and so so happy.

'Does she know who I am?' Noah asked.

'She recognises you, Noah. She knows about the process and realises that she mustn't connect with you physically while you are here. She isn't focusing on Noah, the person. Her reality is purely living out here.' Treigo said.

'There's two, three, four of you living at a given time, Noah, any place, anywhere. There is a lot to keep up with,' Shona said, laughing.

'You are not just one energy in one body. You have separated your energy into various physical bodies across dimensions, so you can experience life from various stand points. It could be their own energy spirit looking back at them,' Ledar added.

They focused once again.

'So I'm in the same time period as before. I'd taken some drugs last night, smoked, and then woke up experiencing a nightmare. I swear I was in hell,' Noah explained.

'Ok, so in this situation, not even we could reach you properly. The connection had been temporarily severed. We could get a glimpse of you, but we were unable to gain communication which is why the higher realm seemed to intervene,' Shona explained.

'Lemme send demionee.' Ledar signalled to end the meditation.

'Sorry about the abrupt ending. We need to go to the chamber so not to reactivate the undesired here. Noah, follow Shona and Treigo; you go get the others.'

Noah gave Triego a confused look. He wanted to know what Ledar had in mind, but then he also didn't want to know it; he was not clear with his thought process.

Noah was led out of the tepee and down the tiny paths through the rainforest. Every track and canopy was lit with lights. The wild animals above could be heard talking amongst themselves. *It was so beautiful here*, Noah thought as he followed the group.

Eventually they got to an opening, and as they looked down into the valley, there was a huge golden Pyrite pyramid so bright that it lit up the night sky. Upon getting closer, they saw the images of Carridion warriors, their native language, and communities carved into the structure. Noah was familiar with it somehow.

'Welcome back,' Shona said as they entered.

'Back?' Noah asked

'Do you remember spending time here before?'

'It does seem familiar. Did I used to come here?' Noah asked.

'Indeed. It's a place of celebration,' Shona replied.

As they entered, Noah could feel that he was in a sacred space. The atmosphere took over his body, and he got goosebumps. The space had a certain charge to it. In front of him were two catafalques side by side on an altar. The others had assembled on seats surrounding the altar.

Noah noticed an opening above. The night sky and stars were visible. He looked around and spotted Treigo walking in with the woman they'd told him was Layla. They approached Ledar, who was nodding at what Treigo was saying.

Ledar began to address the gathering.

'Be seated, everyone.'

Noah and Shona found a seat.

'Now, due to its nature, we need to use other means to clear Noah's energy. Both of you have been brought here because you are one spirit, so what affects one ultimately affects the other. As you know, the walls of this pyramid have Tourmaline, Obsidian, Kyanite, and many more crystals embedded in them which are strong enough to withstand the negative energy imprinted on Noah through Stella years ago.'

Noah turned his head towards Treigo and murmured.

'Stella?'

Treigo shrugged his shoulders.

Ledar continued.

'It came to our attention that black magic was inflicted on Stella when she was carrying Noah. It was casted on Noah's father also, which ultimately led to his death, and it has been creating mental problems in various family members in recent years. The dark entity, which we are reluctant to name, has been circulating. Its insidious nature mainly remains dormant, but at times of weakness, it latches on, causing anxiety, nightmares, bad fortune, and addictions, to name but a few. Finally, leading to what Noah experienced. It's of Subsidion nature.'

The others gasped in disappointment.

'We have engaged our wisest healers and psychics to transmute and clear this dark force; otherwise, Noah's mission will not be successful with this hindering energy. Will Noah and Avia both approach the altar and lie down, please,' Ledar signalled.

Leading the way between the two, Treigo lifted Avia onto the catafalque. Noah jumped onto the other one. As they lay there awaiting the next instructions, Noah looked across at her. She turned to look at him. Staring into her eyes, Noah felt a calm wash over him. He instinctively put out his hand to grab hers, but she moved it away.

'We mustn't touch,' she said.

Noah nodded and put his hand back by his side. She looked straight up towards the sky.

'Are you not scared?' Noah asked.

'I'm never scared here,' Avia said.

'Okay, if you can both remain calm and stay with it. We will attempt to rid the entity from you for good.'

'Please relax,' Shona said.

They closed their eyes.

Four healers, one of which was Treigo, approached the altar. They forwarded their palms towards to two of them to manage the energy. The drums and chanting began.

Noah noticed he felt like he was levitating. He could see the light again. He felt a gentle spinning motion, and his body expanded out. Numbers started entering him as though he was being encoded. 8136, 1111, 1010, 333. He could see the images of Layla being poured into him and then an image of them merging into one. A dark shadow moved into view. Suddenly he felt a pull as though it wanted to hold him down again. His body started jolting off as he felt the reluctance of this entity. Noah could hear the chants, calling upon higher beings and protection. The drumming got more intense. The entity was literally being sucked from his body.

Noah let out an almighty wail as it was pulled out of his mouth. He could feel the dark energy sucking his body up towards the opening of the pyramid. It didn't want to let go of Noah, who felt like he was fighting to get away again. Suddenly his body fell still, and everything stopped.

The chanting slowed down, and the drums quietened. Silence descended.

Ledar signalled the healers to return to the gathering. He moved towards the altar and touched Noah's leg and then Avia's arm.

'When you are both ready, you can open your eyes. Do not rush yourselves,' he said.

Noah felt dazed.

'You ok?' he asked, turning to her.

'I feel fine. Just tired,' she said, smiling.

Noah could see Ledar taking instructions from the others.

'You are now clear, protected, and free to go.' Ledar pronounced.

Noah got off while Treigo came forward to help Avia get off and carried her back. Noah felt like helping her, but he was more than aware not to make physical contact with her.

He walked behind, watching as Treigo carried her back up the paths and through the forest to her holding.

Noah waited outside for Treigo to come out.

'Thank you for taking care of her.'

'Not a problem, brother,' Treigo replied.

'The women are looking after her. Get some rest, Noah. I will take you to your tent; we can meet in the morning before you leave.'

Chapter Ten

Preparing to Leave

Noah woke after one of the best nights' sleep of his life- content and with a feeling that everything was right just as it was. To not have any underlying anxiety about anything felt so nice.

The living quarters here felt manly but luxurious. There was a free-standing copper bath on one side and a metal table on the other side, full of dishes the women were preparing for breakfast. There appeared to be very little privacy around here, Noah thought, but yet it didn't seem an issue to anyone either.

'Hi,' Noah said to the young woman preparing the breakfast and pouring the drinks.

'Hi,' she replied.

'I can help you if you need me to,' Noah said

'Oh no, it's ok, besides there are plenty of women outside wanting to come in here and help," she said, making air quotes.

'Oh, ok,' Noah said, laughing. 'Maybe I'll just get bathed and dressed then.'

'Okay, do you want any help with that?' she asked very innocently.

'Oh no, I'm good,' Noah said, laughing to himself.

Just as Noah got into the bath, Treigo bowled in.

'Brother!' he shouted.

'Jesus does no one knock around here.'

'Knock?' He went back to the opening and sarcastically knocked the canvas. Treigo laughed as he grabbed some bread off the table and headed towards the bath. Noah continued to wash as Treigo perched himself on the edge of the tub.

'Right, Noah, Ledar wants me to get you up to speed on a few last things, so here goes. I'm getting bored with all this backfilling now brother by the way.'

'Ok, I'm all ears,' Noah replied.

'Okay, now keep up. Your Carridion parents made sacrifices so you would become the next Ledar someday. They could have stayed in Carridion indefinitely, but they chose to reincarnate again for the good of this dimension. They had predicted this day would come and paid you a service early on. They saw in you strength and fearlessness that very few have ever possessed. They saw a man capable of expanding ideas but not in the fighting, violent sense; instead, in the power of your connection with us and your level of knowledge in the 3D stream. You have not lost that stream of consciousness as you are of the pure ley lines. What runs through your energy field is so pure that your thoughts are beyond the normal on earth,' Treigo said, making air quotes.

'What is it with the air quotes today?' Noah asked.

'Heh?' Treigo said, confused

'Oh, never mind. Continue!' Noah said. 'And why are you speaking like you're reading from a script?'

Treigo looked confused again and just continued.

'So you have a fierce streak, and your nonconformist ways make you powerful. Yes?'

'Yes.' Noah said in agreement, sinking under the water.

'You are powerful beyond the bliss ever experienced by most, and you have the ability to see out of the box, coupled with your lineage. This is your time, Noah. Are you keeping up?' Treigo said, now walking up and down.

'Yes, I'm keeping up.' Noah said, rising out of the bubbles.

Noah saw an image in his mind of a tall, dark-skinned man with greenish-blue eyes, a scar on his face, and wounds all over his back and arms.

'Oooo, who am I seeing?' Noah asked, knowing that Treigo could see into his mind.

'Monsorrat. Your Carridion father!' Treigo informed him.

'Many lifetimes ago, Monsorrat took numerous beatings across the borders between here and earth before he decided to leave this dimension for good. The Subs knew he had you in hiding; they were trying to get to you eons ago. He endured several beatings before they realised he would never disclose your whereabouts. Eventually, Monsorrat just let go because he knew they'd follow him everywhere.'

'Let go?' Noah asked.

'Moved on to his next existence. Decided he could help you better by being in a different dimension.' Treigo said. 'Now the woman you are seeing, Noah, with beautiful dark skin and long jet-black hair riding a black horse, is Ruma.'

As she slowed the horse and circled, she looked straight at Noah. He could see that she had the most familiar eyes. As Noah looked at her, he felt his heart melt soothingly.

'Your mother lifetimes ago was killed by the Subs. Not long after Monsorrat left because they knew she also would never or could never let harm come to you. They followed her too. Finally, she gave up her position to return to the 3D and be with you there.'

Noah's head dropped in sadness as he felt a hit of emotions, as a human would.

'Don't be sad, Noah. Although she is never able to return here, she lives elsewhere. What you see of her on that horse is not just her. Don't forget death as humans see death is not correct,' Ledar said.

Noah then registered what he'd said about the 3D.

'So she's alive?' Noah asked.

'She is nearer than you think.'

'What do you mean nearer than I think?' Noah asked.

'Noah, your thinking is still bouncing between your human thoughts and emotions and Carridion. Ruma can never die. She has changed dimensions but can and will not die. The Subs have forgotten this as they severed all connections to Carridion and became the darker side. Hence the killings, torture, and destruction in the 3D,' Treigo said.

'Where is she now?' Noah enquired.

Rumar living as a human on earth is actually someone very dear to you.

'Who? Stella?' Noah asked eagerly.

'Roles don't necessarily transfer so identically, Noah. She is actually your sister,' Treigo replied.

'Which one?' Noah asked

'Isla,' Treigo confirmed.

'Isla? She's so irritating!' Noah replied

Treigo smiled.

'Don't ever think for one minute, Noah, that people don't have a say in the whole thing. She made the decision to leave Carridion so that you could evolve to your status with her help. No one ever dies! You are starting to remember now, Noah. You are getting up to speed with us.'

Noah smiled. This news filled him with complete acceptance of a never-ending connection with his family. But then questions started arising.

'So my sister is my mom? That's a bit weird,' Noah said, laughing.

'No, Noah.'

'I know, I know, I'm just joking,' Noah said

'So, who is Monsorrat?' Noah hesitantly asked

'He hasn't reincarnated in 3D,' Treigo replied

'And Stella and Daisy?' Noah enquired, wanting more and more details.

'That's enough for now, Noah. It's not useful information.'

Noah's thoughts switched back to Stella and his sisters on earth. Noah felt a fire rising in his chest. Reading his thoughts, Ledar said, 'Noah, you need to soothe yourself. I know you are feeling human emotion, and you need to get yourself together here first before you can be of help to them. Time is not too much different from where you left it. We are ahead of time here. So Stella is still at home right now. Look!'

Noah shut his eyes and focussed on his family. He saw Stella standing in the kitchen, reassuring Mable, who was behaving peculiarly under the kitchen table. This reassured Noah, and he felt a sense of calmness.

'Life there isn't done for you, Noah. You don't want to stay here permanently,' Treigo said.

'I'm not? I think I do. I don't want to go back there. I want the girls with me and even Mikey, but I don't have any burning desire to go back there,' Noah confirmed.

'So what is it with time?' Noah asked. 'Can thought affect time? I noticed when I was back there that I could make time go faster or slower depending on my attention.' He continued.

'Noah, you can affect anything depending on your focus and concentration. Time is no different,' Treigo replied.

Noah realised everything that now existed revolved around time, and this was reducing man's abilities to think beyond and out of the box. Maybe the future in all its possibilities already existed, and humans were sucked into the now moment because that's all there was. You could create as many possible futures for yourself, but you can only do it from your imagination right now. So if you were to sit and be in that imaginary future situation as you would like it, then you can guarantee that it exists. As the future then already existed, so that too was the past but just not physically experienced. Therefore, the future and past were past. Right now, the present moment was the only time there really was. Each moment creates the next now which leads to the next now, and the chain goes on. Then he thought if the future had already happened in another dimension, humans were actually heading in whatever direction they wanted at any point in time as every moment allowed any possibility. The thoughts that flow to humans at every moment show where they're heading. Then a thought popped into Noah's head.

Reading his thoughts, Treigo intervened

'As well as all that, we never intend to stop communicating with you, know Noah. In fact, there's only been once when you couldn't interact with us. We will never leave you because we are part of you,' he continued.

'So why are you a different idea or voice in my thoughts?' Noah asked.

'Because we are part of your higher self! A higher intellectual form of you that looks only at the most pleasurable outcomes. We are what humans call God, but what we actually are is a part of God, like you!

The happier version is all that exists here!

Noah. You are seeing this all from a human perspective. No one dies; they just move on to different roles and switch to different life experiences, so Isla isn't on earth with you to be your mom his time.

If you are having doubts about returning Noah, stop! You will, and you are going back. In fact, you are the only

Carridion who can cross between these two dimensions, which is why you are the chosen one. You have contracts to fulfil before returning. Home is always here, though, Noah,' Treigo confirmed reassuringly.

'Can you pass me that towel?' Noah asked

'Sure.'

Noah got out of the tub just as one of the women walked in.

'Oh my!' she said, hurrying back out again.

'Carridion has truly blessed you, my brother,' Treigo said, laughing.

Noah smirked.

'I'll see you down at the beach in ten.'

'What can I expect when I get there?' Noah shouted to him as he walked out.

'You have a task. If it succeeds, my brother, it will help many people awaken. Humans have been asleep long enough!'

Chapter Eleven

It's Time

The others gathered on the beach. Noah strolled down, not realising that he was leaving so soon.

'The Subs want to limit your ability to move between earth and here and any prospect of other humans doing it in the future. The only way they can do that is to alter your energy level somehow so that you can't penetrate this dimension. We need to stop them from executing this plan.'

'Our theory is they will try to do it by getting you and others to stop believing and trusting in the process, causing earth's inhabitants to drop further behind in their evolution.'

'Your Carridion self will return. Trust me, Noah!' Ledar said.

'We are hoping that your presence alone will be revered and people will be drawn to you beyond what you've ever known. Your energy is so pure, clear, and therefore attractive. Masses will come to surround you, we anticipate,' Treigo continued.

'Oh, God,' Noah said, feeling overwhelmed.

Your family back there is under lockdown because the government is panicking and feeding off fear. We are aware of some Subs working within the government, too, which are progressing things in that department,' Ledar said.

Noah began questioning the disappearance of planes recently, unexplained loss of memory in people, and increased violence on the streets. The others failed to show any sign of emotion regarding Noah's questions.

'The Subs are responsible, yes. It's not an attack from fellow humans; it's an invasion by our kind. Since breaking away from this stream, they must have penetrated lower-level vibrations. Their only control now is through such avenues.'

Noah felt numbed by hearing that. He now wanted so much to return to Kingsbridge, to the days when he was whinging about going to school. *I wouldn't whinge now,* he thought. He just wanted some normality back. He didn't want this. *Why me?* He thought. His own kind, attacking his humankind. His thoughts went straight back to Stella and his sisters.

'Always appreciate what you have got.' Treigo said, reading his thoughts.'

'Why did the Subs rebel?' Noah asked.

'They wanted power beyond thought. They got ahead of themselves competently. A denial of the Carridion values coupled with their thirst for power led them to dip into lower dimensions and past lives. Eventually, they lost their connection to us.'

'It's not all bad though, Noah, as it will serve all other humans, hopefully. Their seeming wrongdoings will open up an opportunity for humans to see differently.' Ledar continued. We are expecting you to mediate between the humans and Subs,' Ledar announced.

'So if I'm to mediate, who will be with me?' Noah asked.

'No one is going with you,' Ledar confirmed.

'Right,' Noah replied, throwing his arms up in the air.

Ledar laughed at his reaction.

Noah didn't find it quite so funny.

'The higher you get the energy on earth with hope and positivity, the greater the chances for us to step in and help. Until then, it is impossible for us to lower our frequency that low,' Treigo said.

'Bacus, who appears to be the main Subs leader, knows you are the main connection between here and earth, and he knows your abilities. We believe they're invading the 3D to ultimately get to you. The influence that you could have in the world means he wants to try to destroy your energy and come back to lead Carridion. Convincing the humans of who you are will be our first challenge. As soon as we have them on our side, the sooner we can focus on weakening their hold on things,' Treigo said.

'Believe me, Triego, humans are not going to listen to me, and I don't remember this Carridion stuff enough,' Noah said.

'You will by the time you're back there,' Ledar said.

'Basically, the Subs have been morphing into humans and causing destruction on epic scales by embodying the elite, people who work for governments or media. Your job is to get people on your side and get them to only focus on the positive outcomes, not fear or worry. That way, the Subs can't easily penetrate. Keep your expectations high and positive – the lesser negative thoughts, the better.

Noah turned to Treigo.

'They are moving around quickly via telepathy, so the moment they locate you, they will regroup and appear there.'

'That's ridiculous! How will I know who they are if they are using metamorphosis?'

'Noah, we are a thought away. You need, above all else, to keep your faith and the signs we'll send you. Feel your way through, Noah.'

'I need a few minutes,' Noah said

'We have very little interim time now, Noah,' Ledar said

'I need a few minutes,' Noah replied as he headed back up into the village.

Seriously, what the fuck are they asking me to do? Noah thought. Noah continued to walk for a while, and as he looked up, he saw Avia walking down towards him.

As they approached one another, they both slowed down.

Standing a foot away from one another, Noah stared at her, and she at him. Her energy was just the same as Layla's. And he felt exactly the same standing in front of her as he did when he was back in the 3D. Like a compulsion, Noah went to touch her but then pulled his hand back. They both knew that physical contact was not allowed in this realm. She smiled at him, and at that moment, Noah knew. He knew he had to go back for her and them.

She stared at him with joy and delight in her eyes, both knowing what the other was thinking. Without speaking,

Noah turned around and reluctantly headed back to the beach. As he turned back around to get one more glimpse of her, she'd gone. Noah smiled to himself. He knew she had appeared at just the right moment, and he knew he couldn't fail the task ahead.

Noah walked back onto the sand.

'Noah!' Treigo said, grabbing his hand.

'I'm ready!' Noah declared to them all.

Ledar nodded.

'I'm ready!'

Treigo hugged Noah while Ledar tapped him on the back. Noah headed into the sea. He took one last look of Carridion before turning around, focusing on earth, and diving back into the water, immediately entering the tunnel of light.

Suddenly he was standing in his familiar Kingsbridge surroundings but this time as a Carridion. Noah looked around at the desolate quayside and felt panic rise inside at the eerie feeling that the lack of human life created. He realised that the lockdown was still in place. The only noise around him came from the squawking of the seagulls, who seemed to be telling Noah that they were scared too.

Noah shook his palms at the gulls.

'Sssh, it's okay, guys.' Surprisingly, they seemed to respond by quietening down.

Noah looked round for something to cover himself with as he stood bare-backed with just an animal skin hiding his modesty. As a Carridion on earth, he felt huge. His stature was larger, and his bare feet probably resembled a size 15 compared to his usual size 10. His hands were big and strong, and his legs were long and muscly. Due to his strength and speed, he headed up the hill to his home in as little as a minute and with no effort whatsoever. Noah started to feel powerful, but as he got nearer to his house, he felt a wave of anxiety. How the hell he was going to be able to convince Stella and his sisters who he was, he thought.

Noah sat in the garden staring at the house for a while. Birds were going mad in the trees because of his presence. Mable approached him and started to bark.

'Mable, it's me,' Noah said, putting his hand out for him to sniff. He started wagging his tail once he realised and nudged his head alongside Noah's leg. Noah stroked his head lovingly.

'Well, at least you recognise me now. That's a good sign,' Noah said.

Stella looked out of the window to see what Mable had been barking at. Noah was behind the bushes. He rubbed his fingers on the bush next to him. The smell reminded him of his childhood. For a moment, the smell made him feel the innocence and calm of a five-year-old.

It was nearing dusk, and it appeared time had stood still on earth whilst Noah had been gone.

Stella was standing in the kitchen talking to the girls about the lockdown, but then he heard her saying to Daisy, 'You need to go and wake Noah soon as he won't sleep tonight.'

Noah needed to get a move on before they tried to wake him. He decided that Daisy was the best bet for helping him. He knew she would recognise him, and so he needed to get her attention and out of the house.

Noah waited for her to enter the lounge and then tapped on the patio door. Daisy looked up from the television, but couldn't see anything, so she turned back. Noah tapped again. She walked up to the door and opened it.

'Is that you, Mable?' she asked.

Noah grabbed her arm and pulled her outside, shutting the door behind her. She wanted to scream but he put his hand over her mouth. He led her over to the cherry trees. He looked straight into her eyes. She stared at him, shaking but mesmerised by his green eyes. She noticed Mable was acting all excited and rubbing up against his legs.

'Daisy, it's me, Noah.'

She squirmed and tried to scream.

'Daisy, please, it's me. I need you to focus. I need you to help me.'

She continued to stare into his eyes. Somehow she instinctively knew it was him.

'I'll release my hand if you promise me you won't scream.'

Daisy nodded. Noah slowly removed his hand, and she unhooked her arm from his grasp and looked at him from head to toe.

'Noah, what the fuck?' she said.

'I know! I have a lot of explaining to do, but I don't have much time.'

'But Noah, you're upstairs in bed. You're a boy, not this,' she said, waving her hand up and down at him.

'If you go upstairs, you will see my body lying there, but you wouldn't be able to wake me. My spirit is here, and I have returned as a Carridion.

Daisy, earth has been invaded, and it's going to leak soon. Plus, they are coming after me.'

'Who are they?'

'A breakaway group called Subsidions. It's likely they are going to be disguised as humans. They have already been doing this. They like to disrupt people's thought patterns with propaganda and scaremongering. What they want is to keep lowering the frequency so that they can control people and stop them from evolving. They also want to lower my vibration to keep me here so they can try and take over Carridion, where I come from. It's a long story!'

Noah and Daisy turned towards the house as the doorbell rang. Noah crept to the kitchen window to see two policemen at the door talking to Stella. Noah had a bad feeling. It then occurred to him that they weren't real police.

'Daisy, quick! Get back inside and start screaming that I'm not breathing.'

'Ok. Where are you going to go, Noah?'

'Just go in, please. Oh, and make sure you give my phone to Mikey somehow, as I'm going to need it to stay in contact with you.'

Daisy ran in and started screaming on the stairs. Noah made his way round to the front of the house. He saw Stella shut the door on the police, and they got back into a car.

Noah followed the car down the road and noticed they were turning towards the cottages.

Noah's heart started to beat fast.

'Stay focused, Noah,' he heard Treigo whisper.

'Oh my god, Treigo, you made me jump. They are going after Layla, aren't they? Why, why would they go after her?' Noah asked.

'Just protect her, Noah. Layla and the baby are better off out of there.'

Noah stopped in his tracks.

'What do you mean, baby?'

'The child she is carrying, Noah. She is a Carridion in nature and will be the next chosen one.'

Noah froze.

I got Lay pregnant the other night. Last night, whenever it was now. How so, he thought.

'Do we need to reply to that, Noah?' Treigo asked.

'No, don't!' Noah replied as he scaled the trellis at the side of Layla's house and climbed onto the extension roof. He looked down and watched as her dad answered the door to the Subs and spoke to them for a few moments before inviting them in.

Noah tapped on Layla's bedroom window. She pulled up the blind but couldn't see anyone. As she opened the window, Noah pulled it further open and climbed inside. Layla went to scream, but Noah put his hand over her mouth.

Why is putting my hand over girls' mouths all I seem to do here?

'Stop, Layla. It's me, Noah!'

Layla struggled, and Noah pinned her to the bed and sat over her.

'You need to listen, I'm not who I normally look like because something has occurred,' Noah said

Somehow, Layla wasn't as fearful as someone would normally be if, say, any stranger piled into the bedroom. Like Daisy, she intuitively recognised something about him.

Layla continued to struggle, though, and her heart was beating fast.

'Calm down,' Noah said.

She looked into his eyes and he felt her relax beneath him. Noah released his grip and removed his hand from her mouth. They just stared at each other for a few moments, Noah put his hand on her face. Noah smiled and got up from her. Grabbing both her hands, he pulled her up onto her feet.

Layla stood staring at him. Even if this wasn't a reality, she didn't want to question him being there with her. They could hear talking downstairs, and they both looked towards the door.

'We need to get you away from here because those guys downstairs are not who they appear to be. You are in danger, especially now.'

'Why Noah? And why are you looking like a twenty-seven year-old and dressed like that? I don't understand,' Layla asked, confused.

'I'll explain more later. But please just come with me.'

'Get away from me,' she said, pushing him.

Noah didn't move an inch and Layla just fell back onto the bed.

'Lay, I'm not kidding,' he said as he grabbed her back up off the bed and held her hands. She recognised his touch and voice.

Before she could even reply, they heard her Dad coming upstairs, followed by the police.

'Layla!' he shouted.

'You need to trust me,' Noah said. Grabbing her and flinging her over his shoulder, Noah focused intently on getting them away from there. He closed his eyes and used what he had learnt back in Carridion.

'Have faith in the vision,' Treigo whispered in his ear.

As Layla's Dad pushed the door handle and entered the room, he found the window open and the curtains flapping in the breeze. Noah and Layla found themselves standing safely on Black Sands beach.

The sea was out, and there was a faint glimmer of light from the nearby café that was still open.

Noah had never used his full Carridion powers before, and even he was shocked that his vision had worked.

'Bravo, Noah,' He could hear Treigo saying.

'What just happened, Noah?' Layla asked.

'Why am I now standing on the beach?' she said looking all around her.

Noah stood upright, still trying to get his breath back. Molly looked up at him properly this time. He was much taller than usual. He took her hand and turned towards the café at the top of the beach.

'Noah, can you please put some clothes on? You look like some sort of caveman.'

Noah looked down at his half-naked body and laughed.

'What is this anyway?' she asked, tugging at the animal skin tied around his waist.

'Catskril, a native animal! Well, a dead native animal now, obviously.'

Noah looked around at what he could maybe do about clothing, and over in the distance, he saw a garden encroaching onto the beach.

'Ok, let's head this way first,' he said.

He looked at Layla and felt so pleased to be with her again. Time felt so distorted. He felt like he'd been away for months.

Noah ran over to the garden at the top of the beach and jumped over the small white picket fence. He grabbed a t-shirt off the line and ran back to Layla on the beach. He looked at her face as he squeezed into it.

'I know you're confused, but please stop giving me that look.'

Layla just looked at him and then turned away to look at the ocean which was shimmering in the moonlight.

Noah put his finger underneath her chin and directed her face back towards him.

'Look me in the eyes,' he said.

Layla wouldn't look.

'Look at me,' he said again.

She looked directly at him.

'I don't have time to explain all of this right now, but it is me, and you need to trust me right now.'

Layla studied his face and kind of recognised the similarity again.

Noah touched her tummy.

'Layla listen, I'll explain. I had to leave. I was forced to really. If it had been my choice, I wouldn't have been able to cope with it. My mission is to help Carridion, which is why I am here like this now with you. I got pulled back to Carridion the night of lockdown whenever that was. Sorry I've lost all track of time.

They told me I couldn't be in contact with you for a while. It wasn't that I didn't want to be, it was that I couldn't be for my sake and yours and, well, basically all of humanity apparently, which just sounds too epic really for one person.'

'What do you mean you're here to save humanity? Have you been taking drugs again, Noah? Because if you have…'

'Ssshhh, no, not at all. Please don't make me feel helpless about all of this as I do already.'

'So what are you saying? That I don't know this Noah now?' she said, waving her hand up and down in front of his body.

'Why does everyone keep waving their hands up and down at me?' Noah asked.

'Who else has seen you like this?'

'Daisy. She has helped me already,' Noah replied.

Noah grabbed her wrist and moved her arm to the side.

'Layla, most of this has been out of my control and now I am this part of myself which is my fuller version.'

'Oh my god, I don't understand,' she replied, pulling her arm away. 'I feel sick,' she said, stumbling back.

Noah leant forward to grab her.

'Show me your birthmark on your thigh,' she said

'Oh yeah, look, here,' Noah said, showing her.

'Hurting you hurts me too,' Noah continued.

'Okay.'

Noah led her to the empty café. The staff were clearing away and getting ready to shut for the night. The woman inside looked over her glasses at them as they entered and scooted onto the corner table.

'I need to get Mikey's help,' Noah said. 'He has some bravery, and I need help with what needs to be done.'

'What needs to be done?'

'I'm going to have to listen to the guides who are giving me messages, but I think I need to figure out who the Subs are disguising themselves as. I think it's trustworthy normal citizens as well as people in authority. You need to be protected too, lay.'

'Why? What have I done?'

'Nothing.' Noah thought it was best not to tell her that she was pregnant right now.

They sat in the cafe for a while thinking of a plan. The waitress came across and asked them to leave soon as they were closing up.

'Come on, let's get you to Mikey. He'll take care of you whilst I can't.'

As they headed back down the beach Noah held her hand and thought about Mikey's, and suddenly they appeared at the end of his drive. Mikey had a huge house nestled in a woodland on the outskirts of Kingsbridge. He had once told Noah that the fact his parents had so much money had made his life worse. He truly believed that if they hadn't been so rich and work-focused, he would have been happier.

Layla went up and knocked the door. Only the side lights from the porch made anything visible. It was nearing ten o'clock now, and Layla could hear Mikey's parents discussing who it could possibly be. He answered the door.

'Layla, you ok? Come in!' Mikey said, ushering her in the door.

Noah watched from behind the trees as she entered the house, and shut the door behind her. Layla explained to him that Noah needed a favour and that she needed to stay there. Noah felt happier knowing where she was, but he knew he needed to now get back to Stella and the girls. He took a few deep breaths and focused on what to do next. Running back to the main road through the woods, his speed got so fast he could barely feel the ground. The earth and him became almost one. Suddenly his body lifted, and suddenly he found himself rolling across some grass. He came to a halt just before entering the holly bush, and on looking around, he discovered that he was in his own garden.

There was an ambulance outside his house. He could see the lights flashing down the alley. They had obviously come to take his body as, by now, it would only be showing a faint sign of a pulse. Treigo had told him that when his spirit was in Carridion, only a small amount was left in the human body, which was enough to just keep it alive. Noah hated that he was putting Stella and the girls through such distress, but he needed them to play out the plan; otherwise, nothing could be done.

Noah hid behind the holly bush for a while, trying to focus on what to do next. Treigo's voice appeared.

'The Subs are disguising themselves as the authority, so the only way forward is to penetrate their infrastructure.'

'It does appear they are morphing themselves, which means the public trusts them. I'm going to have to let myself be known.' Noah said in an uncertain, questioning way.

'Noah, you clearly don't look or act human, so it won't be hard,' Treigo said, laughing.

'Treigo, it really isn't a laughing moment,' Noah said, amazed at how laid back he always was.

'There can always be a laughing moment, Noah!'

Just as they were speaking, an explosion went off in the distance. Noah jumped to his feet.

'It's the electrical substation out of town, and from what it appears, they are about to target the gas plants too,' Treigo confirmed.

'Are they planning on starving the people out until they conform?' Noah asked.

A second explosion went off. The ground shook, and it was as if time stood still for a moment. Noah could hear screams from inside the houses and children crying.

Very few people were coming out of their homes. Too scared by the warnings and what might happen next. The few that did see Noah run past just looked on in disbelief and muttered to one another before quickly going back into their houses. They no doubt thought it was an invasion of a new species, but Noah didn't have time to explain, so he continued to bolt towards the substation about a few miles away. He could visualise the Subs swarming all over the area. Rifles in hand, dressed in police uniform. Noah felt it was time to make himself known

He imagined himself on top of the roof near the substation, and suddenly he was up there staring down at the commotion. He could see the fire engines and ambulances approaching from the distance. Noah shouted down from the roof.

'You!' he said, pointing at the tall Sub below. He locked eyes with Noah, and he quickly turned to aim his rifle at him. Noah moved away as two more uniformed police officials ran from around the corner and looked up.

'He's up there,' shouted one of them, and then the bullets began to ricochet off the roof. Noah ran and lunged onto the adjacent roof that was partially ablaze. It had loads of chimneys rising from the power station below. He looked down to see them running up the stairwell at the side of the building. Noah knew they would be able to withstand the fire because they had the power to, so he wanted to keep them close until the emergency services arrived. If he could get the public to see that these policemen were not normal, they would question who they were.

Noah squatted down behind one of the chimneys. His heart was pounding with both fear and adrenaline. He suddenly started to panic as negative thoughts started to flow through his mind. He started to feel like the young, insecure nineteen-year-old that he also was and started to panic about how the fuck he had got himself in this. He looked down at his arm as it held onto the metal chimney. It had beads of sweat on it and the veins were protruding and scars were visible all over them from past encounters as a Carridion. In that split second, he realised he wasn't that young human boy anymore, and sadly he would never be that person again. In that moment, he also knew there was no way he could not do this. This was his way forward and what he was alive to do, and in that split second, he fully accepted that he was a Carridion Warrior. Noah went to get up when Treigo whispered;

'Noah, stay low. I'm watching where they are.'

Noah trusted his brother and stayed crouched. He could hear footsteps just a few metres away.

'Noah, you may as well come out and end all this craziness,' the Sub said.

'Noah, don't move,' Treigo said.

The sirens got louder and louder. Noah could see one of the Subs look down off the rooftop. He heard trucks pulling up, creating more commotion below. He could see the Subs boots pacing in front of him just a metre away.

'Noah, we can do this the easy way, or we cause bloodshed,' he shouted.

Noah heard Treigo's voice in his head as clear as though he had shouted it to himself.

'Run, Noah. Run!'

'Why can't I imagine myself out of this situation, Treigo?'

'Because they need to see you leave. Possibly think that you are dead. That is more important right now to you, so your thoughts won't work like that at the moment.'

Noah stood up and ran in the only direction possible, towards the explosion site. He was aware the Sub had spotted him and knew he was drawing his rifle to shoot him.

'Run, Noah!'

'What into the fire?' Noah said in his head.

'Trust,' Treigo said.

For fucks sake! Noah thought as he took the leap of faith.

Their bullets fell into the fire as he ran towards it. They could barely get near as smaller explosions were still occurring. Ironically, what they caused, now prevented them from getting nearer to their desired target. Noah stood in the middle of the fire, totally unaffected by the heat. It was as if he had a shield around him that was keeping the flames a distance away.

'Get yourself out of there,' Treigo said as Noah stood without as much as a hair on his head being singed.

Noah could see telepathically the Subs eagerly greeting the fire service down below.

'You are now completely up to speed with Carridion,' Treigo said.

Noah closed his eyes and imagined himself back at home, and within a split second, he was back at Coppice. No one was there as Stella and the girls were now at the hospital with his barely functioning body. Noah stood and thought about what to do. He gathered some food in a rucksack and some tools out of the shed. A blanket and torch and headed for the woods. He knew he could spend his night there without being found and could take some time to think about his next move.

Before dealing with that, he had one more important thing to do. He grabbed a pen and paper, jotted some things down, and left it on the table next to his bed.

He gathered his belongings and headed to the woods.

Noah made a fire and sat there staring at it. Then he realised that his thoughts and the flames were in sync. The more he allowed himself to become one with the fire, the more the flames danced and soared to provide answers to his thoughts. When he asked if the Subs were near, the flames kind of lost energy; Noah took this as a no. When he asked if Layla was safe with Mikey, the flame soared. The messages were very clear. He trusted the verification received in the fire form.

'The flames are right, Noah. The Subs aren't that close at the moment. They are still trying to work out why your body isn't in the fire. It seems that they have lost so much connection that they can't get answers to things quickly. They no longer trust in the universe, so they are definitely going to take a while,' Noah heard Treigo saying.

Noah was sucked out of his mesmerised state and became quite startled by Treigo's presence next to him. So much so that he nearly fell off the log he was sitting on. Treigo laughed.

Noah laughed.

'My nerves are fraught already, brother.' Noah said, grabbing Treigo towards him to hug him.

'I thought I'd visit you to tell you you're on the right path so far, my friend.'

'I thought you couldn't cross over, Treigo,' Noah said.

'As you have fully realised your potential, it seems it has given me more manifesting abilities. So I asked Ledar if I could cross over, and here I am. I just hope I can make it back,' he said, laughing.

'You need to go to St. James Church soon.'

'St. James Church?'

'Don't forget that whatever presents itself to you is a sign or message. Everything, Noah!'

As Noah turned back to look at Treigo, he was gone.

'Fleeting,' Noah thought.

'I just wanted to try it out, Noah,' Treigo said, laughing.

Noah thought about the church. He knew of it and knew the Father there as he was quite a revered figure in Kingsbridge. He knew that it was a safe haven. Father McManus would definitely protect him for a while and help keep his identity secret. Noah decided if the Father could stall them whilst he planned his next move, it would allow him some extra time. Noah was pretty sure the Subs would kill anyone to get to him, but they would think twice before killing a man of the church. Armed with this knowledge, he headed to the church on the hill.

The church sat at the top of a small hill in a very picturesque setting overlooking the town. Noah paced up the steps to the oversized open porch area. He stood in front of the oval oak door and pulled on the bell rope in the corner. He noticed he was now protected from the fierce wind and rain pelting him a minute ago on this oversized porch. He felt comfort from this alone. Noah realised that he valued the feeling of being at ease right now.

A thin pale lady in old-fashioned clothes and a flowery apron that looked as old as her eventually arrived at the door. She looked up at Noah, who was towering way above the door frame, and her face went into an even slighter shade of beige. She looked behind her, trying to attract someone's attention, but no one was there.

Noah could feel her anxiety and tried to reassure her.

'It is okay. I'm not going to hurt you.'

But as he put his hand out to touch her arm, she stepped back. It was then that he realised his hand and arm looked huge in comparison to her small, frail body. Noah then stepped back.

'My name is Noah. Can I speak to Father McManus, please?'

The Father appeared from out of one of the doors down the corridor. The lady shut the door on Noah, but he could hear her muttering to the priest. He could hear the Father reassuring her, and then the door reopened. He stepped aside, put his arm around Noah's back, and ushered him in while peering outside before shutting the door. Noah watched as the Father slid two large metal bolts across the door.

He looked up at Noah, who smiled at him, but he didn't return the gesture. He just kind of muttered under his breath. He then walked up the corridor very quickly, making the sign of the cross and saying, 'God help me.'

'Can you ask him to help me too whilst you're there?' Noah said, laughing.

The Father, just kind of, nodded at Noah who continued to follow him down the dark wooden-clad hallway and into one of the rooms.

Father McManus was a small Irish man in his late sixties, early seventies. Noah felt he'd lived in Kingsbridge for a very long time.

Noah was led into a dark room filled with even more wooden panelling. There were bookcases from floor to ceiling brimming with literature. Noah was directed to sit at the large oval table. It reminded him of one of the large tables he sat around in Carridion, although that one was made from ad hoc wood from fallen trees. *Much prettier,* Noah thought. This one was perfectly lacquered to almost mirror effect.

The Father stood next to Noah's chair and looked him up and down.

'So, son, where are you from?' he asked.

'A place called Carridion,' Noah replied.

'Are you indeed! Are you here to help or hinder us?'

'I have pure intentions. I'm not here to harm,' Noah replied.

'There are certainly some strange things going on right now. People are very scared,' the Father said.

As he was speaking, the frail, pale lady walked back into the room with a tray of tea and biscuits and looked at Noah out of the corner of her eye as she put it down on the table. Noah felt amused by how English people thought tea was the solution to everything. He thanked the lady, but she just ignored him and walked out. Noah laughed to himself.

'So Noah, what's going on?' the Father asked.

'Okay, the world, but here especially, is being penetrated by a breakaway group. They are after my dearest people and me, but essentially they intend on taking over as they want control.'

Father McManus thought for a moment and then walked towards the bookcase. He realised it was quite high up, so he signalled Noah to help.

'Do you mind?' he said, slightly embarrassed that he couldn't reach it.

Noah grabbed the large leather-bound book the Father was pointing at and handed it to him.

He frantically flicked through it at the table, clearly looking for a particular page. On finding the page, he thrust it in front of Noah.

'Look! Look!' the Father said, banging the page with his finger.

Noah looked at where the priest was pointing.

It read; on the first day, there would be explosions. On the second and third days, harmful things will rein down from the skies. People will fear for their lives and those of their children. On the third day, darkness will fall, and life as we know it will diminish under the rule of the dark spirit. On the fourth day, the course of life may change and but the only retribution will be if positive force prevails. For this to happen, the majority must show unity and love of life and one another.

Noah looked at the priest, who was almost the same height as him, whilst he was sitting. The Father was hovering next to him and almost bouncing from one foot to the other in anticipation of Noah's response.

'Well? What day are we on?' the Father asked.

Noah stood tall. Bending over the table from his height was just awkward, and the chairs were too small for his frame.

'Well, it seems this must be why I needed to come to you, and we're on day one.'

'So, what are you going to do, Noah?'

'What I'm going to do, Father, is to gain the trust of the people, starting with Kingsbridge. The media should do the rest,' Noah said.

'Let me help you, son,' the Father said lovingly that ensured Noah he had him on his side. Noah bent down a bit, looked into the Father's eyes, grabbed his hand, put his other one on top of it, and shook it. He grabbed the book, smiled, and walked out towards the front door.

'Noah,' the Priest shouted.

Noah turned back to look at the Father.

'I will head down to the town in the morning and call for the locals to explain who you are and what's happening.'

Noah nodded.

'Explain that I'm here to help, and please remain positive, Father. No negativity! Positivity speeds up energies and time; negativity slows things down. Because the Subs are struggling to keep up with this time-space reality, it will work in our favour if we speed things up through positivity.'

As Noah carried on walking, he remembered something else.

'Oh, please tell people not to let anyone into their homes if possible. Not even the police.'

'Not even the Police?'

'No, Father. Not even them.'

'Now I am confused,' he said, shaking his head.

Noah felt he was now in a position of strong power. One built on trust with the Father!

He looked at the housekeeper standing in the hallway. This time she looked up at him, grabbed his hand, and kissed the top of it. Noah smiled, unbolted the door, and headed out back into the harsh weather, back to the woodland where he could best channel his thoughts to what he should do next.

When Noah got back to the camp he'd set up, he started seeing images of firework-type explosions falling from the sky. Pounding balls of light and people running everywhere. He didn't think it was England but somewhere in Greece or around that area.

He knew this was a premonition of what might happen. He thought about what the Subs had put in place to make this happen. He focused on the flames again, which were roaring. In his mind's eye, he saw harmful gases being catapulted from wind turbines across the country.

There were, of course, all possibilities in the future. The key was to focus on what humans wanted to happen now, not what they didn't want.

Eventually, Noah noticed the sun coming up and breaking through between the trees. It was a beautiful sight. He could almost forget where he was and what was going on for a minute. It was so peaceful in the woods. Everything felt still. This alone made Noah feel how special earth was and the reason why it was worth fighting for. Forgetting reality was probably the best thing he could do if he was to remain positive, he thought.

Noah's thoughts turned to his girls. He focused on them in his mind's eye and saw them sitting next to his bed in the hospital. Daisy was telling Stella that all was going to be fine. He could see Stella was staying strong and positive, which comforted him.

Noah picked up the book the Father had given him, thanked the woods and the fire for guiding him and keeping him safe, and headed towards the main road. Noah thought the best thing to do was to head to the village hall in Kingsbridge and introduce himself. When he reached the top of Diamonds Hill, he could hear the Father already speaking to hundreds of locals through a loudspeaker that had been rigged up outside. The media had turned up and were filming everything from the top of the hill. Noah could feel the anxiety and anger spreading throughout the congregation as a result of fear. He walked through the crowd, and silence transcended. He entered through the open double-arched doors into the hall. Gasps and whispering began as people parted to let Noah through to the front.

The Father spotted Noah and relief fell over him. Noah smiled at him as he stepped up onto the stage. Noah put his hand on his shoulder and patted it with respect and reassurance. He passed him the mic. Noah just stood there for a few moments looking out at the people. They all sat staring at him, some mumbling amongst themselves about who he was. As he absorbed the energy, he could feel their fear and anxiety drop away. Noah's energy was such that the most frightened and angry beings were calmed and healed by his focus. He was now in a position of channelling negative emotion, filtering it like impure water. Purifying all the atmosphere in that room and beyond, Noah felt people relaxing. He looked around, still not speaking. He spotted Layla and Mikey near the back of the hall. His heart began to race slightly as he realised how much love and protection he felt for all these people and the enormity of what he was doing. He took a deep breath and focused.

'I know you look at me, standing here with my large and unusual-looking body, but please don't judge me on what I look like. I'm a Carridion which means I don't just come from here.'

'What do you mean you don't just come from here?' a male voice shouted from the crowd laughing.

'I was a human, some of you will know me as Noah Emins, but I'm no longer just him. In fact, I've never just been him. I've taken my Carridion form back, and I may never return to this 3D as a human again.'

Noah sensed Layla's pain as he spoke these words. He looked over at her, and her head dropped in sadness. He stared at her, urging her to look up at him, and after a few moments, she did. He smiled at her, and feeling reassured by him; she gingerly smiled back.

'Who are those who are taking over, which we keep hearing about?' a lady asked from the back row.

Noah turned his attention to a woman who looked a lot like Stella.

'They are a breakaway group called Subsidions. They are here to kill me, sever my connections, and take control of humanity by intercepting your thoughts. Penetrating the most influential with mass fear disguised as protection and goodness.'

A woman who stood in the middle of the crowd with long red hair and pale skin raised her hand and said in a gentle but strong voice.

'So what can we do to help, Noah?'

People turned to see who had asked the question. The sunlight shone through the stained glass window above the main doors and straight into his eyes. Noah quickly closed his eyes and turned away. He thought for a moment and realised this was a sign, and then words began to flow.

'I need you all to focus on what you want. Respond with as little fear or anger as possible. Without a response, the Subs are less likely to be able to keep a hold on human energies or manipulate through hysteria.'

The Father then grabbed the mic from Noah.

'The sky will turn blood red, and things will reign down if we don't get a hold on this. I know this to be true.'

'Okay, thank you Father, you're not helping.' Noah said, swiftly grabbing it back off him.

The crowd started getting anxious, and loud mumbling ricocheted around the room.

'Things like what?' one man shouted.

'The Subs will blast something out in the skies, so you will then need to keep yourselves, your children, and animals safe,' the Father continued.

'Okay, okay, calm down, everyone. Father, you're not really helping, mate.' Noah said. The priest nodded and backed away. 'As I've said, positivity is the key. Not letting them get into your heads with fear like now.'

'How are we to stay positive when we are scared?'

'Look into your loved ones' eyes, preferably children's, and see that love in them, that calmness. This is the type of thing that will keep you trusting. We are not just of this earth plane. We are all destined for other things in time.'

'Are we to stay indoors?' an elderly lady asked.

'Cellars, bunkers, caves, houses, anywhere like that, but yes, definitely indoors,' Noah said.

People started to walk out of the hall.

Noah caught Layla smiling at him. Her face beamed with pride for him. He smiled back at her and winked. Noah then looked at Mikey; reading his thoughts, they both nodded at one another. Mikey quickly led Layla out the main arched doors at the back.

'It's time for me to get going, Father,' Noah said, handing him the mic and pulling him close for a hug.

The crowds got up and started hastily moving out of there.

Chapter Twelve

Getting On

Noah entered a cave nearby Blackpool Sands. Bending so as not to bang his head, he walked to the back and sat down. He chuckled, recalling Mikey saying, 'O.M.G Noah, you are massive,' as he squeezed his bicep.

Noah noticed how cold and damp it was. It was okay for him, but he certainly wouldn't be inviting Layla there anytime soon. So from here, the luxury of the Mancave, Noah realised he would have done anything to be in this cave as the younger human Noah but now that his thoughts had produced the goods, he wasn't so sure it was so exciting. He'd much rather be lying on a warm beach. *Well, isn't that just the way it goes,* he thought.

So Noah thought about the next plan of action. He focused and saw the Subs lining the streets of Kingsbridge, patrolling all the way to Salcombe looking for him. He could feel that they were getting impatient and angrier. He wondered if giving himself up was the best option. Less stress for everyone, and it would take some of the anger off the streets, he thought.

He messaged Daisy to see how the people were.

'They're not that happy since you haven't reappeared, Noah. Most are defending you and staying positive. A few are saying you are maybe just a weird-looking bloke from somewhere. A loon, they're saying.'

'Okay, that's fine. I'm not concerned with being seen as a weirdo. I'm more concerned with the vibe of the people.'

'No, generally, people are positive. Neighbours are all chatting amongst themselves. They're calm! But we want to see you, Noah. Everyone does, I think.'

'Okay, I'll have a think. Is mom still oblivious to what's happening back in Kingsbridge?'

'Yeah, she's still here at the hospital. She hasn't left your bedside.'

Noah knew if the Subs weren't able to find him, they would start hurting other people and causing mayhem, as the book had predicted. They were determined as they were so far on the dark side that they had nothing to lose. Noah decided to lead them towards the cave, away from everyone. Focusing on them and sending them images of where he was through thoughts, he could see them in his mind picking the signals up. Noah lay on the floor, drifting in and out of sleep, waiting for them to discover him.

It wasn't long before they reached the cave. Noah got up as they approached.

'I'm coming out,' he shouted.

Their head torches were blinding him, so he was treading carefully as two of them came forward and dragged him out. There must have been at least another four of them standing outside. Even though Noah came calm and unarmed, they still proceeded to drag him all the way back up the cliff. The front of his feet scraped on the stony path and they kept deliberately dropping him on his knees. They wanted notoriety for what they'd achieved. They wanted to reassure the people that their man had been caught.

As they led Noah up onto the streets of Kingsbridge, locals came out and watched. His blood poured down from the front of his legs. His hair was no longer tied back but dishevelled and falling over his face. He looked like he hadn't washed for days. His eyes were still as bright and piercing as they'd always been but he looked tired.

As the people started to gather, gasps began radiating, and it wasn't at the disgust of seeing Noah, but it was seeing how he was being manhandled and the damage they had done to him. One stepped out from the crowd.

'Please, there's no need to be hitting him like that. Let him walk!'

The Sub pushed him back so hard that he fell onto the gravel. The public started following as they passed, unnerved by the attitude of these so-called police.

Stella and the girls gathered outside. They'd left Noah at the hospital and returned home when they heard that they'd been explosions and trouble on the streets. Still, with no idea that it was Noah that was involved, she ran over.

'Let him go. You can't treat him like that,' she said.

'Leave it,' Noah said, looking his mom straight in the eyes.

Stella felt jolted.

'Why are they doing this to you? Is no one going to do anything?' she screamed.

Some were scared, and some people were keen on remaining calm as they'd been told; they felt unable to intervene. Isla ran over and told her to come away.

'Mom, I have something to tell you,' Isla said.

At that moment, Stella's mobile rang.

'Miss Emins, you need to return to the hospital immediately,' the voice on the other end said.

Noah lifted his head as he saw them head away from him back up the hill. Isla turned to look at him. She felt at a loss for what to do. Follow her mom or stay.

As they led him to the main square, crowds followed. The Subs were intent on making an example of him.

'Mom, look at the police over there?' Isla said, pointing.

'They've sussed on to what's going on down here. That lad will be ok. Come on girls hurry, we need to get back to the hospital.'

Isla felt an impulse to go over to them.

'They're not real police who have him down there.' she said

'Isla, Daisy come on now,' Stella said even more angrily.

'I can't,' Daisy said. 'He's my brother.'

Stella stood staring at Daisy whilst the information sunk in.

'I need to go down to him,' she shouted.

'Madam, we're just getting confirmation on this as we speak,' one officer said to Stella.

The radios started going berserk as they heard one say that no police officers had been dispatched from Totnes.

'Oh, fucking hell!' one officer shouted as they all started running back down to the main square.

The police grabbed their weapons and signalled to one another. They had already been tipped off about certain individuals posing as law enforcement.

'Mom, I need to tell you something,' Isla said.

'Not now, Isla. I need to get back,' Stella said.

'Mom, Noah is here. That's him down there with them. We can't leave.'

'What are you talking about?'

'Look, look at my messages,' she said, showing Stella Noah's messages over the last few days.

'He's not at the hospital. Well, at least his soul isn't,' Isla explained.

Stella felt she knew what was happening and she quickly made her way down to the square. She pushed her way to the front to get a glimpse of him again.

'Stand back, get back,' the police were shouting.

Some of the police were down on their knees, ready to fire at the Subs, but they had Noah held in front of them. She looked at Noah's face, covered in blood, and shouted out to him.

They caught one another's eyes for a moment. Noah held her gaze.

'My dear boy!' she said

'Stay focused, Noah,' Treigo whispered.

Noah took himself to another place in his mind. He was half here and half back in Carridion, swimming in the ocean again. What the humans were seeing wasn't what Noah was experiencing. At that moment, Stella sensed this. She stared at Noah and pride flooded towards him. They both shut their eyes and focused themselves away from there.

The police continued to try and talk the Subs down. Helicopters had started circling above. Out of the side of the helicopters, rifles pointed at the square. Noah hoped they wouldn't react with violence, but as he focused on what he didn't want, he heard one Special Forces Officer shout;

'Let him go, or we will fire.'

One of the Subs who was holding Noah just laughed. 'Do you know who we are? Do you?' he shouted.

'We don't care who you are. You are not doing this!' he replied.

The crowd began chanting Noah's name.

The crowd got louder and louder as they moved out of fear and anger into strength.

Noah shut his eyes and listened to the people calling his name.

'Noah! Noah! Noah! Noah!

At that point, he wanted to retaliate and use his power to get them off but something was stopping him. He knew it wasn't the time for that. Stella looked around, and as she did so, she shivered with goosebumps. She knew, at the moment, the power of Noah; he was transforming thousands at that precise moment. Everyone was feeling it pulsing through their bodies.

The Subs knew they were losing control. One went to raise a metal bar at him, but the crowd just got louder and louder.

Noah wasn't going to react violently. This would go against everything he was. He shut his eyes and felt the strength of people's support and returned it back to them.

'The crowd is winning, Noah,' Treigo said

'I know this is what needs to happen, Treigo. I know people need to feel their own power again and what feels right and good. I know I could use my power of attraction to get out of here, but the people need to rise,' Noah replied.

Noah knew he had to remove himself and the Subs from the situation but not in front of the people. He knew to stop the violence from escalating, he needed to go with them. The Subs were edging over towards the riot vans.

'Let them take me,' Noah shouted to the officer in charge.

He looked at Noah and could tell he needed to let them go. More bloodshed here wasn't advisable so he commanded his officers to stand back as they bundled Noah in the back of the van. The van sped off towards the landfill areas outside of town.

The helicopters turned on themselves and began following. People ran back to their homes to watch the news which was now being broadcast live from the cameras above. The people watched as Noah was beaten with batons and kicked repeatedly. Thoughts of Layla, Stella, and the girls, kept running through his mind. Noah kept entering in and out of Carridion. He felt life leaving his body. The pain was there, but it wasn't what humans would think of being beaten to death.

Kill me, Noah thought. It's a far easier place to be, and you lose all that power you think you have then. Do it, he thought, but every time he was just about to opt out of the human realm, he felt compelled to stay a while longer.

'Perfect timing, perfect timing Noah,' Treigo whispered. Reassuring him that the impulse to go will come when it comes.

Sweat and blood ran down into Noah's eyes, stinging as it made contact with his eyeballs.

Noah spoke to Stella telepathically.

'I'm fine, mom. Please don't be sad.' Noah said.

Noah knew the minute he moved back to Carridion, the Subs would follow him out of the earth plane.

Growing weaker as he slipped from this illusion called earth, drifting into the other dimension, he felt he couldn't maintain his connection much longer and was starting to opt out.

'When the power is surrendered completely, everything will flow, Noah. The outer will change,' Treigo said. 'Noah, not yet. Not yet,' Treigo repeated in his ear. He could feel Ledar, and The Others stood waiting.

Treigo knew where and what was going on with Layla and the girls, and if he could keep him on the earth plane a bit longer, things would pan out better.

The Police followed along with Stella who had made herself known. Intent on making him suffer, they watched as the Subs dragged him up an embankment, the sun now scorching his bloody skin. Remaining at a distant they positioned their weapons and Noah became unavoidably in the firing line.

'Drop your weapons. This is your last chance or we will open fire.' The main commanding officer shouted across with the megaphone.

As they engaged the weapons, suddenly the daylight changed. Everyone automatically looked up. Noah, just managing to lift his head, saw hovering above; one spacecraft after another surrounding what can only be described as the mother ship. It spread lengthways beyond where the eye could see. The detail of these silver crafts was immense, and their silence whilst hovering made it all the more awe-inspiring. It wasn't loud or threatening but quiet and calm.

'Cavalry has arrived.' Treigo said to Noah, laughing with such excitability. Noah could feel Treigo's joy.

'Who are they?' Noah asked through thought.

'It is us. Carridion. The future!' Treigo said.

'Are you on that?' Noah asked.

'I'm here, Noah. The shift you've just helped create in people's thinking has allowed for it.'

The crafts continued to hover for what must have been about ten minutes. Just watching. Watching the people. Watching Noah.

Their presence and appearance was enough. The Subs had already let go of their grip of Noah and retreated back to their vans. Suddenly a dust of smoke could be seen and they were gone.

No one cared. They were insignificant right now.

Noah could feel himself drifting away from this existence. He wanted to be on the mother ship now with the others. His time here was done.

An armed police car drove Stella over to Noah and as she approached him she fell to her knees at the sight of him. Lifting his head off the floor and stroking the back of his hair, she cradled his injured Carridion body. Tears ran down her face. She could see he was slipping away. His eyes kept shutting, and as much as he was trying to focus, his conscience was drifting in and out.

She leant over him and whispered into his ear.

'Go, Noah. Go to them!'

And he slowly shut his eyes for one last time.

Chapter Thirteen

The Letter

To My Girls -

If you're reading this, it's because they've come for me, and I wanted to go. Please don't let this make you sad; it's just that my time is done here. You need to remember girls that I'm never far away. I'm certainly not lying on that bed in my room. I'm here in your thoughts. I'm sitting next to you. I'm walking beside you, stroking your faces, and sending signs to you all the time through my thoughts.

Please speak to me often and let yourselves see the signs I'm sending. Trust that you are feeling, hearing, and seeing me as we are always together! You will feel me before you see me again, as you are part of me, now and always.

Look after my other girls, Layla and Mikey and the one growing inside of her. Give them lots of love and affection from me often.

I'm happy where I am because I'm home, and until we see one another again in person, please be happy whilst in the 3D. Remember, it's not what everyone thinks it is. It's all just a big play ground really!

I love and appreciate you all & remember you are forever free!

Noah

P.S. Burn my bodies. The land is for the living, and fire helps dispel the energy.

Ingram Content Group UK Ltd.
Milton Keynes UK
UKHW020746250723
425746UK00015B/463